CONTRARY TO POPULAR BELIEF

COLD
CALLING
DOES WORK!

VOLUME II   EFFICIENCY, THE SCIENCE OF APPOINTMENT MAKING

CONTRARY TO POPULAR BELIEF—
COLD CALLING DOES WORK!

VOLUME II EFFICIENCY, THE SCIENCE OF APPOINTMENT MAKING

iUniverse, Inc.
Bloomington

Contrary to Popular Belief Cold Calling Does Work!
The Art & Science of Appointment Making
The Science - Volume Two of Two

Special bulk discounts are available to corporations, professional organizations, and other organizations. For information, please contact the author at bcaponi@caponipg.com or by phone at (817) 224-9900.

iUniverse books may be ordered through booksellers or by contacting:

iUniverse
1663 Liberty Drive
Bloomington, IN 47403
www.iuniverse.com
1-800-Authors (1-800-288-4677)

ISBN: 978-1-4620-0498-0 (sc)
ISBN: 978-1-4620-0500-0 (hc)
ISBN: 978-1-4620-0499-7 (e)

Printed in the United States of America

iUniverse rev. date: 05/17/2011

Contents

ACKNOWLEDGMENTS

Many of the books I've read over the years have started with the authors making what sounded—to me—like self-serving comments about how difficult they found writing their book. So now that I've completed my first book, I find that I'm no different—and only now can I truly empathize with them.

When my wife, Nancy, and I started our sales training and consulting business at the beginning of 2004, I found that I loved to write, so I've been blogging and writing articles right from the beginning. Piece of cake to compile that work into a book, right? Trust me; it is not as easy as one might think.

The reason I bring that up—other than perhaps also appealing for the *sympathy vote* myself—is that I have many people to thank for helping me on my odyssey.

First of all, I must thank my sister, Deb Newman, for being the first to suggest that I write a book. She has been after me for a long time and has never given up on me—although she must have thought about using a very large stick from time to time to get me to do it!

I also must thank my wife, who put up with the very early mornings, late nights, and long weekends away from her and the things we like to do together (even when on vacation) that it took to get it done.

Thank you to my good friend, Bob Howard, founder and president of Contact Science, LLC, whose brainchild, Klpz, is the science of the Art & Science of Appointment Making. So many times he helped me take my thoughts and put them to paper in a more concise manner.

Thanks to my colleagues and good friends Stu Schlackman and Steve Bregman, who took the time to read this book and gave me solid feedback—as well as one of my best friends, author Richard Merrick, who also invested a lot of his time to do the same.

Lastly, thanks to my brother Todd, who actually was the one that got me into this business that I love. Thanks to you all.

FOREWORD

Sales are the life of every company. Without sales, we don't exist—period. Every company's number-one concern when it comes to selling is what's in the pipeline this month, this quarter, this year, and how will we improve our position to make our budget.

There are many excellent books in the market today that tell us how to interface with the prospect or with our existing customers. They focus on strategic selling, questioning techniques, presentation skills, and how to close the deal. The problem is that there is not much out there that addresses the most important and toughest job in sales: getting new face-to-face appointments with new prospects. There is a huge difference between pipeline management and pipeline building. Selling truly starts with appointment-setting, and that's where successful sales professionals invest the right amount of time and effort to ensure success in improving the size of their pipeline.

Barry Caponi is the expert in the sales industry when it comes to appointment-setting. He has been training world-class sales organizations for the past decade to better understand the art and science of appointment-setting. Barry's approach is the authoritative source when it comes to improving the effectiveness and the efficiency of the challenge, and this book is a great reference manual for his methods. Even though there are many great lead-generation programs today and excellent tools for referral marketing and networking via social media, sales organizations still need to make calls to set appointments. Barry has developed a methodology that will get anyone more appointments.

As a sales trainer who has written two books on selling and has spent twenty-five years in the selling arena, I can assure you that this book addresses the entire set of tools, processes, and skills that are needed to be successful when it comes to a salesperson's biggest fear: *the cold call.*

Whether we are seasoned sales professionals or just starting out, this book is a must-read for any of us who are interested in building a robust pipeline that leads to success in selling year after year. Barry knows the challenges sales professionals face and his ColdCalling101™ *formula* is one that works—regardless of whether calling warm leads or cold names. I use it for my own business. Enjoy his approach as he addresses this facet of selling in a very practical way!

Stu Schlackman,
President of Competitive Excellence and author of *Four People You Should Know* and *Don't Just Stand There, Sell Something.*

WHY SHOULD I READ THIS BOOK, OR WIIFM (WHAT'S IN IT FOR ME)?

WHAT IS THIS BOOK ABOUT?

This book (and its companion, *Volume I: Effectiveness, the Art of Appointment Making*) is about the business process of getting enough targets *into* the pipeline through the discipline of telephone prospecting (even if we begin the process by canvassing door to door).

Let's face it—very few of us like to cold call, and many of us actually claim that we don't do it at all. In reality, however, most of us go through the process of asking strangers for appointments every day. We just don't call it cold calling. To illustrate that point, I've included a blog in this book that addresses this in detail. It's entitled, *There's actually no difference between a cold call and a warm call.*

This set of two books is about three things: defining the business process of appointment-setting, explaining why the process is necessary for almost all sales professionals, and showing how to do it more *efficiently and effectively.*

THE IMPORTANCE OF THE DISCIPLINE.

Two salesmen who haven't seen each other in weeks meet in a coffee shop for lunch.

"How's your day?" asks the first salesman.

"Great! I'm following up on several good leads. I've got a great prospect I'm working with—and I'm waiting on a PO from another client."

"Yeah," says the other salesman, "I haven't sold anything today either."[1]

There are three morals to this story.

1. Conversations like this emanate from an empty pipeline.

2. A continuing flow of closed sales comes from a full pipeline—and a full pipeline comes from a continuous flow of Initial Appointments.

3. "Make no mistake," I said in *Is Cold Calling Really Dead? Searching for the Elusive Silver Bullet*, "at the end of the day, whether the call is cold or warm, it almost always falls to one of us sales professionals to pick up the phone and dial the number that starts the dialogue that begins the buying process."

What this somewhat humorously attempts to point out is that the ability to set the Initial Appointment that begins the selling process is a critical process to all of us in sales. What it doesn't point out is that it is typically a neglected process. We like to say that it is the elephant in the sales bullpen. Everyone knows it's there, but because no one knows how to solve it, we just gingerly step around it.

Case in point, there are several books and websites out there today devoted to the concept that cold calling doesn't even work—or that it has become an obsolete or unnecessary discipline. (You can find some of them in the Other Resources section.)

If you read through the literature from those who say cold

calling is obsolete or dead, you'll find a common theme: replace cold calling with pull marketing programs designed around technology and other activities to eliminate the need for it. Ideas such as website optimization, staying in contact through newsletters, e-mail, networking, and asking for more referrals from our existing customers are good ones, and they all work. As a matter of fact, we do them all and suggest that we all do as many as make sense in our own organizations to cut down on the number of cold calls that our teams must make. But here is the reality: if these pull programs don't generate enough Initial Appointments to fill the pipeline, we must still cold call. And, for the majority of us, they don't and we must.

For most of us in sales, the selling process begins with what we like to call an Initial Appointment. Initial Appointments may be face-to-face, over the phone, or through a web-based technology, but somehow or another, we've got to convince people (we call them targets) that it is in their best interest to open their calendar and make some time for that first meeting with us.

Here's what you need to know about this process. There are basically three sources for an Initial Appointment with a target. They are:

1. Lead-generation marketing campaigns that are designed to get people to raise their hand and tell us they are interested (this includes traditional advertising such as print, TV, radio, and direct mail, plus newer approaches such as social media);

2. Networking and referrals; and

3. Cold calling

But here's the rub with lead generation and referrals: just because someone expresses interest in our solution through one of our marketing programs doesn't mean that we'll get the appointment every time we call for one. Even strong referrals tell us no in exactly the same manner that cold call recipients do—they're just nicer about it because they don't want to offend the person who referred them to us. In other words, *the process we follow when asking for an Initial Appointment is exactly the same—regardless of whether the call is warm or cold.*

Therefore, the *skills, tools, and processes* we need to call marketing leads, to follow-up on referrals and networking connections are *exactly the same* as the ones we need to cold call. That also means that almost everyone who is charged to find new customers—or even expand his or her presence within existing customer accounts—must be able to *efficiently* and *effectively* set appointments.

WHO IS THIS BOOK WRITTEN FOR?

I've written this book from the sales manager's perspective. But what if you're not a sales manager? What if you're a small business owner, independent sales professional, or sales professional reporting to a sales manager? This book is also for you, because—like it or not—God has given us all the ultimate equalizer or a level playing field, if you will. It's defined by the same number of hours in each and every day. Those of us who are more *effective* and *efficient*, win. Those of us who are not, lose. It's as simple as that. And need I remind anyone that there are no monetary awards for second place in sales.

So regardless of whether you have responsibility for managing a team or just yourself, this book will have something in it to help you and/or your team become more *effective* and *efficient* at the business process of filling the pipeline.

WHO IS BARRY CAPONI AND WHY SHOULD I LISTEN TO HIM?

I have been selling my entire professional career. I've sold computer hardware and software solutions, property management services, life and health insurance, and of course the speaking engagements, sales consulting, and the training services I now sell.

All of these require mastering the business process of prospecting and appointment-setting. So not only have I been studying this process since starting my company in 2004, but I've had to set appointments to get those buying cycles going throughout my entire selling career.

I've been a sales manager at every level—from a front-line district sales manager to chief sales officer of a global company. I've had to manage sales professionals who also had to set appointments to get those buying cycles going. In those jobs, my main concern each day was about the insufficient and poorly qualified pipelines that I was being presented with and how to consistently fill them.

I've also personally sold solutions that required me to call at just about every level of management; as the price tags on what I was selling ranged from just a few thousand dollars to millions of dollars. Of course, when selling life and health products, I also called upon individual consumers in addition to businesses.

I hope that this helps you answer, "Who is Barry Caponi?" However, what about, "Why should I listen to him?" Since founding the Caponi Performance Group, Inc., I've concentrated our focus on this business process of helping our customers consistently get more targets *into* the pipeline. But why did I choose to concentrate on that instead of the more traditional sales training curriculum of helping get prospects *through* the pipeline?

That one is an easy question to answer since I had no desire to make our job any more difficult than it had to be. Sales managers have consistently told us that, once in front of a target, their teams were pretty good at scoring runs—to borrow a baseball analogy. (This has not always been true, but that's a story for another day.) There are also many excellent methodologies and sales consultants available today to help in this more traditional segment of the selling process.

I decided to concentrate our efforts where our targets believe their biggest barrier to success has always been—getting enough "at bats." Therefore, since we already had one of the very best methodologies for improving the *effectiveness* of setting appointments, (***The Appointment Making Formula™*** or as we affectionately call it, ***The Formula***), and had also found the best and most unique tool[2] in the market to improve the *efficiency* of the process, why not concentrate our efforts where there was the most perceived pain? Therefore, our brand—ColdCalling101™—was born.

Since there are a lot of very good methodologies out there to help us take prospects *through* the pipeline phase of selling, the key question we asked ourselves when first addressing this challenge was why it continues to be so difficult for sales teams to get targets *into* the pipeline.

Our research and experience with our customers led us to conclude that the answer to that question was that everyone has been operating under a basic and *mistaken assumption*—to get quality targets *into* the pipeline, we can just use the *same skills, tools, and processes* that work so well to move a prospect *through* the pipeline. After all, selling is selling, right? (See blog entitled *The skills that are necessary in the pipeline phase of selling are not the same as those required in appointment-setting.* As for the issues involved in the *effectiveness* side of the process, they are addressed in Volume I.)

The result of this mistaken assumption—the application of the traditional pipeline-selling approaches to the challenge of setting appointments—has proven to be both *ineffective* and *inefficient*. For instance, many companies tried to address *efficiency* by using the same CRM, contact managers, and sales force management applications that they use to help them drive prospects *through* the pipeline. Other companies tried to address just their *effectiveness* challenges by applying the same scripting and objection-handling approaches they use in the pipeline. When neither approach succeeded in consistently feeding the pipeline, most sales managers fell back on the traditional mantra: "Make more dials!"

In reality, the primary goal is relatively simple—to achieve the required number of Initial Appointments with as few dials as possible in as short a time as possible. Yet the accomplishment of this goal is obviously not so simple.

So here's why you should listen to us. We've studied this portion of the selling process extensively and:

1. To our knowledge, our ColdCalling101™ solution is the only all-encompassing approach to meeting the appointment-setting challenge (e.g., we supply all the *skills, tools, and processes* of appointment-setting);

2. The tool (Klpz) we recommend was specifically designed to address the different challenges of the appointment-setting process;

3. The skills (*The Formula*) are also designed just for the appointment-setting process;

4. We provide tools for the sales manager that they've never had before—and we teach them how to use those to be a more effective coach and manager; and lastly

5. The use of our solution will *sustain the gains* over a long period of time.

Adopting the ColdCalling101™ approach has transformed many a sales team's whole approach to prospecting. As a matter of fact, those that do implement our methodology routinely double or better the number of Initial Appointments that their sales team was setting prior to using our comprehensive approach.

Additionally, as this book is written from the manager's point of view, let me take a moment and expand on the one element on this list that applies to us as managers since it is critical to the success of any implementation of our solution and it is what makes the inevitable gains sustainable.

We have provided managers with a more powerful set of tools and reports than we've ever had before. This is accomplished through the *science* (a tool called Klpz from a company called Contact Science) that allows us to see the entire process in all of its component parts, and provides the tools and processes for managers to easily *monitor, measure, and manage* it through quantitative metrics.

The first challenge for managers in the appointment-setting process has always been the lack of credible, accurate, or timely information. For example, many of us ask our sales professionals for the number of Initial Appointments that they set each week. Or perhaps we additionally ask for the number of dials that they make to set those appointments. How many of us believe what's in those reports? In our experience, the answer is a very few of us.

The disbelief in those numbers is not based entirely on what we might think, though. Sure, some of our lesser-performing charges fudge (I'm trying to be politically correct here) those reports, hoping to buy time to catch up. But there is also the undeniable truth that it is difficult to keep up with the data that goes into those reports. Anyone who has tried to keep track of the number of dials, conversations, voice mails left and returned, plus appointments set each day can attest to that. We get interrupted, people return calls when we're out of the office, we make calls from the road, we go from call to call with no time to record the results of the last call, etc. There are many reasons why those reports are inaccurate at best.

However, since we must make management decisions based on something, we make do with the information we've got. Those that are familiar with the old expression, "Garbage in, garbage out," know the dangers of doing so. So the major topic we'll cover here in Volume II is how to improve our underlying data—and how to turn it into manageable information.

A final note: this segment of the sales process is constantly evolving. For instance, technology (voice mail and e-mail in particular) has changed the landscape of appointment-setting over the past five years. And, while the approach we teach will work today, we encourage you to always be fine-tuning as your landscape changes. To help with that, I encourage you to sign up to follow our Tweets (announcing the topic of that week's blog) on Twitter (www.Twitter.com/ColdCalling101), visit www.ColdCalling101.com/blog, and watch for us on www.YouTube.com/ColdCalling101 to keep up with more on the skills, tools, and processes necessary to be successful at appointment-setting as they continue to evolve.

HOW DID THIS BOOK COME TO BE?

As you might imagine, many of my customers have been clamoring for me to publish a book for quite some time. They tell me that the workbooks their teams are provided during our Prospector's Academies™, although great learning tools during the academy, just don't have enough of the detail of what we covered to act as stand-alone reference tools somewhere down the road.

I've also had a number of colleagues who provide sales consulting in the pipeline phase of the selling process encourage me to do so as they also see the logic in our approach (not to mention the results in some of our joint customers).

All of that got me to begin writing a blog on this topic (www.coldcalling101.com/blog) back in July 2007. I generally publish one a week, so I've written quite a few over the years.

Lastly, it has come from two points of frustration with some of those others trying to provide competitive solutions to what we offer—or worse, an alternative panacea to the challenge. We've already agreed that very few of us like to cold call. So why would anyone want to make this process any more difficult than it inherently is? Yet, at best, that is exactly what many of these solutions do—using those ineffective techniques just makes the task more difficult and frustrating. At worst, those that say cold calling (and therefore also by association, the need for appointment-making skills) is dead are misleading sales professionals to believe that they do not need to master this process at all—and that is an immense disservice. Sadly, not one of them has replaced the need for sales professionals to know how to pick up the phone and be both *effective* and *efficient* at the process that begins the selling process. As a matter of fact, this bad advice has probably cost some good sales professionals their jobs over the years.

Here's the latest example of the latter category: the advent of social media. I can't tell you how many sales managers and sales professionals told me in 2009, when sites such as LinkedIn, Facebook, and Twitter became mainstream, that they didn't need our services anymore because they were going to be using social media to get those Initial Appointments. The reality is that social media, at worst, is a time-waster and at best is just another warm lead generator where good appointment-setting techniques are still needed to convert them into appointments.

At the end of the day, we sales professionals are the ones who are *ultimately held responsible* for getting in front of enough targets to make our number. And, regardless of the target being warm or cold, we need to master the skills that are specific to the business process of using the telephone to set an Initial Appointment.

At last count, I had nineteen different books on cold calling and appointment-setting sitting on my bookshelf, so I eat, drink, and sleep this stuff. Of those nineteen books, there are only three (see Other Resources at the back of the book) whose methodologies and techniques I agree with in some form or fashion. In other words, most of the stuff that's out there doesn't work in the long run. The reason that they seem to in the short run is that almost any process will work when we do find those few targets that are *in the market* when we call them. Also, any consistently applied process is better than just *winging it* as most sales professionals have been doing for years and still do today.

The ones I disagree with are all based on the same foundation. They spend an inordinate amount of time trying to perfect the ideal opening *pitch* that will immediately *wow* the target into believing that they just have to meet with us. Then when the target still says, "No," they attempt to overcome the no with logic. At this point, logic has not yet entered the target's mind.

Since most of our targets don't believe that they are *in the market* for what we're selling when we call them, those logical approaches do not work as well as we think they should. Most of the negative responses have little to do with reality or logic since they are nothing but what we call *conditioned knee-jerk responses* designed to get us off the phone. Therefore, logic doesn't work very well until we can get them past that first panic reaction of, "Oh shoot," (fill in your own word there if you don't like *shoot*), "another sales professional! How am I going to get rid of this one?" (See blog entitled *Top ten biggest mistakes cold callers make on the phone* for more on how and why our approach works so well.)

CONCLUSION

I don't expect this book—even combined with Volume I—to answer *all* of your questions. But I do believe that it will give you hope that there is an overall answer out there to the challenge in general and will answer most of the most common questions we hear. As a matter of fact, I'd love to hear about your successes as you apply the answers you do find here.

There are two more resources that you have access to if you are of the *do-it-yourself* ilk. I have written two white papers that are available on my website at www.caponipg.com. One is a senior management paper that describes the challenges of the entire process and describes what the alternatives are. It is called: *Is Cold Calling*

Really Dead? Searching for the Elusive Silver Bullet. The second is more of a how-to white paper that describes how to actually write the scripts for the opening and explains how we handle the, "no," we invariably hear. It is called: ***The Appointment Making Formula™: The Secret to Setting More Appointments.***

Both, by the way, are free. However, if you're like most of our customers and don't have the time it takes to implement a comprehensive program yourself, I'd be remiss if I didn't offer our assistance to help your team double or better the number of Initial Appointments that they are setting presently just as our customers do every day.

If you'd like to figure out exactly what that would do to your bottom line, check out the Sales Activity and ROI Calculator page on our website. You can also find a description of what we do and how we do it there as well.

But regardless of how you proceed, I wish you success in all your endeavors and thank you for the opportunity to earn your business.

To your prospecting success,

Barry D. Caponi

HOW TO USE THIS BOOK AS A REFERENCE MANUAL

The purpose of publishing these chosen blogs is to allow you to quickly find and read a tip on a topic that may be of current concern. The alternative was to force you into reading an entire book on a methodology in order to find that useful nugget of information to solve that particular concern. In other words, it was designed to be used as a *reference manual*.

For instance, let's say that you're having a hard time getting your team motivated to make the calls to set those critical Initial Appointments. They always seem to have an excuse for not getting around to making them and you'd like some help in that area.

Here's what you would do. Go to the Contents pages and look through the blog titles. Depending on the way your charges are stating their reluctance to making those calls, you might find the following entries of interest to look at to determine how to solve this dilemma.

- *Priorities and the need to set appointments.*
- *How many Initial Appointments do I need?*
- *How to rid ourselves of those dreaded dry spells?*

- *Eight simple ideas to help sales management fix an empty pipeline.*
- *Five simple rules to keep calling activity levels consistent.*
- *Making some minimum of cold calling dials each day adds up over the year.*
- *How can we assure we have time to make calls?*
- *Why goals are important in cold calling programs.*
- *The value of making just* one more dial *in a Call Block.*
- *Is the, "Make more dials!" mantra the best way to set more cold calling appointments?*
- *Cold calling is a great predictor of sales to come.*
- *How to motivate sales teams to cold call in a tough economy.*
- *Five tips to help make that first cold call of the day.*

CHAPTER 1:
GENERAL TOPICS

General topics include subjects that are important to understanding the challenge of appointment-setting in general, but not quite pure art or science.

For instance, we cover the importance of appointment-setting, whether it is really necessary, the top ten mistakes that sales professionals make when attempting to set appointments, why the skills, tools, and processes that work in pipeline selling don't work in appointment-setting, etc.

It is a good primer to understanding how we view the challenge of appointment-setting. It is also a great primer to help you understand why your teams struggle at this step in the selling process.

THE NEED FOR PERSONAL IMPROVEMENT.

Sharpening the saw. Are you a member of the 4-4-4 Club for this year yet?

In *The 7 Habits of Highly Effective People*, Stephen Covey addresses renewal and self-improvement in the last chapter. He calls it *sharpening the saw.*

The term 4-4-4 Club is not Covey's, but it still hits the mark. Each of the three numbers relates to setting annual goals for sharpening the saw.

- Read 4 books each year
- Listen to 4 CDs each year
- Attend 4 seminars each year

Lastly, we should be investing 3 percent of our annual income back into ourselves.

Congratulations on making the effort to read this book. Did you know that less than 10 percent of all sales professionals will do anything this year to improve themselves? How are you and your team stacking up on the remaining suggestions?

We hope that our websites—www.coldcalling101.com, www.caponipg.com, and www.contactscience.com—will help fulfill your requirements in the area of sales improvement! As I mentioned in the Introduction, sign up to follow me on Twitter/ColdCalling101 to be notified about each week's blog topic. It will help you quickly determine whether the topic is something that is of interest to you.

IS COLD CALLING REALLY NECESSARY?

Very few of us like to cold call, so how do we figure out whether we need to cold call at all?

It's really a pretty simple process as there are basically only three sources for an Initial Appointment with a target. They are:

1. Lead-generation marketing campaigns that get people to raise their hands and tell us they are interested
2. Networking and referrals
3. Cold calling

To figure out whether we need to cold call (and how much if we do), follow this formula:

1. How many Initial Appointments do I need in a year to hit my sales goal? (You can use our Sales Activity and ROI Calculator that you can find on our website www. caponipg.com or send me an e-mail at book@caponipg. com.)

2. From that number, subtract the following:
    a. The number of Initial Appointments we get from marketing programs
    b. The number of Initial Appointments we get from networking activities and referrals from customers

3. Whatever gap there is between the number we computed in Step 2, subtracted from the result in Step 1, is the number you'll need to fill with cold calling. There is no other alternative.

Two last caveats:

1. Cold calling works best when we do it on a consistent basis, so we must figure out how many we need on average and do some *every* day—or at least weekly.

2. Marketing, networking, and referrals can sometimes not generate what we expected—or an economic downturn can cause us to need more. Make sure you're looking at your results each week to see whether you need to open the cold calling spigot to make up the difference. Did I mention that there is no other alternative?

THE NECESSARY SKILLS IN THE PIPELINE PHASE OF SELLING ARE NOT THE SAME AS THOSE REQUIRED IN APPOINTMENT-SETTING.

There are four key differences.

Many sales managers that we talk to operate under the assumption that because their sales team—once in front of a target—can move that target through the pipeline effectively, they are also properly equipped and capable of getting a target *into* the pipeline. After all, selling is selling, isn't it? The sale—or objective—is just different in the case of trying to set an Initial Appointment, right?

Unfortunately, the answer is no. And this misunderstanding of the differences has created what we like to call the *elephant in the sales bullpen*. It is apparent to everyone that enough Initial Appointments are not being set, but the root cause is not pursued. Instead, sales managers ignore the elephant and utter the old mantra, "Make more dials!"

This four-part blog explores the four major differences: the Beginning Repartee, the Pace of the Exchange, the Types of Responses heard from the target, and Preparation to Succeed.

1. *Beginning Repartee.* If our target has agreed to an appointment with us, the opening moments of the call, although perhaps not yet openly friendly, are at least collegial or warm. That happens because our target has already determined to invest time with us so they are open to the conversation and to us.

   On a cold appointment-making call, the opposite is true. They have not yet agreed that there is value in even talking—let alone meeting with us (even on a referral call). The reasons for that are twofold. The first is that they don't think that they need what we're selling yet, so why would they *need* to have this conversation? The second reason is that we're interrupting them from doing something—so they don't even *want* to talk with us. The result is that they'll do anything, including *lie* to us, to get us off the phone. Hence, the term *cold call* as the target's behavior towards us is cold. What that means is that the call begins as being *adversarial*.

On the Initial Appointment, the normal conversational skills that we all have developed throughout our life are at play. Not so on the cold call. The skills necessary to counter that initial negative response and get the targets to open their minds for a moment to a conversation about how our value proposition has helped others—and hence potentially them—are not needed or practiced in the pipeline half of the selling process.

2. *Pace of the Exchange.* When in front of a target in a sales call, the pace of the conversation is generally deliberate, calculated, and measured. When the target asks us a question, we can take a moment to think about the question before answering. It is totally acceptable to do so. As a matter of fact, it can be misconstrued as a sign of disrespect if we don't ever seem to take a moment to think about what is asked and always seem to be quick with what could be taken as a *canned* response.

On an appointment-setting call, the pace is accelerated. Our targets generally answer very quickly by falling back on their favorite *Conditioned Knee-Jerk Response* (i.e., their typical way of getting sales professionals off the phone quickly). They don't need to think about it—it is a reflex.

We must respond just as quickly—or we risk being hung up on or being put on the defensive. The whole conversation is conducted at the speed of a Nolan Ryan fastball. So if we're not practiced at handling the few standard negative responses that we hear consistently, we'll not have near the results that we'd like or need.

3. *Types of Responses.* Because a target has agreed to meet with us, he or she is willing to hear our story and share his or her own to help determine whether it makes sense to move forward with us. This means that the target's responses to our questions are more apt to be based on logic.

On a cold call, the responses we generally hear are more of a knee-jerk response designed to get us off the phone. Many times, those responses are not even true, although they may contain a grain of truth. If you'll think about it, each of us has our own favorite we use when cold called.

Applying logic to targets' lies does no good because there is no logic in their response. Therefore, when we call people, we must give them a vehicle to retreat from that opening knee-jerk response in such a way that they save face and open their mind to a short conversation regarding what we've done for others to address a challenge or supply a benefit.

We must *counter* their negative response, using a transition that provides them the ability to save face (a lot of our customers felt the same way) and then ask a question that will open their mind to a short conversation by asking one of our *Bridge Questions*[TM3]. (By the way, our counter technique works just as well when the target actually gives us a true response.)[1]

4. *Preparation to Succeed.* When in front of a target during the pipeline phase of the selling process, our preparation for the meeting should definitely include some planning. However, we cannot plan for all contingencies. That means that much of our success is based on our ability to

think on our feet since each situation is at least slightly different.

On a cold call, there are only a few responses that we'll hear if we deliver the same message each time we approach someone. To accomplish that, we must internalize or memorize our opening approach to limit the responses we'll hear and also internalize or memorize the responses we'll use to counter those. We'll also need to practice them so that they roll off the tongue like normal conversation.

TOP TEN BIGGEST MISTAKES COLD CALLERS MAKE ON THE PHONE.

1. Believe the first negative response that we hear.

There are only two ground rules our targets play by when they receive a cold call and we ignore them at our peril.

When we place a cold call, we must understand that the person we're calling really doesn't think they *need* to talk to us. As a matter of fact, our surveys show that less than 5 percent of targets in any sales professional's universe of potential customers *believe that they are in the market* for what we're selling when we call them.

We must also understand that we are interrupting our target from doing something when we call, so they don't *want* to talk to us.

The result of those two rules is that they will do anything, *including lie to us*, to get us off the phone. Most cold calling methodologies teach us to counter their statement using a logical argument (or power benefit) to convince them that they should meet with us. But if they're lying to us, why would we think logic would work against a statement that is not true?

I don't know about you, but I don't have enough time to make calls until I find that 1–5 percent that is currently *in the market*. Since half of them seem to be too busy right then anyway, we must employ a different approach to get them past this *knee-jerk* reaction (we call them negative responses or conditioned responses) designed to get us off the phone before we can apply any kind of logic to their response.

The most powerful technique of ***The Formula*** is called the *Bridge Question*[4]. This concept is what differentiates us from all other appointment-setting methods. It is used to accomplish any one or more of the following objectives:

1. Most typically, it provides us the ability to *bridge* from the target's conditioned knee-jerk response (negative response) into an open minded, albeit short, conversation to share what we've done for others (our value proposition);

2. Provides us the ability to expand on our value proposition, which will help reduce no-shows and cancellations;

3. Should they ask us a question (which we must answer), it *bridges* us back into control of the conversation; and

4. Qualify if desired.

Here then, are the rules (or tests) for the application of *Bridge Questions*. Each question has a specific purpose:

1. It should get us an answer to help qualify the target and get them into a *short* conversation to build value for the meeting;

2. It must call for a relatively short answer;

3. We must be able to predict and control the answer with, "That's exactly why we need to get together. How *is* Tuesday at 2:00?"; and

4. Generally, open-ended questions that qualify as *how*, *what*, or *why* questions work best.

Here's an example of one of the best I've seen:

"How many months of home care could your current financial portfolio absorb before it would begin to affect your retirement plans?" This *Bridge Question* is used by one of our long-time customers, Newman Long Term Care, out of Minneapolis, Minnesota (one of America's leading experts on long term care insurance, by the way). They use it to counter the "I don't need it," negative response that they hear more often than any other. The typical answer is, "I don't know," which is why it is so successful—the sales professional can then respond with passion and belief, the response shown in point number 3, above.

5. *Tell the target all about what we can do for them.*
Remember that they don't think they need what we're selling, so why do we think this approach will work? Instead, we should tell them about the results someone else got from using what we sell. (All of us—okay, maybe just most of us—think that everyone else knows some little secret that we don't that's made them more successful than we are.)

There are three steps to defining the message and then a very simple *formula* to apply it.

• Write out the best success stories of someone using our solutions we can think of. Include these five components:
   a. What were the challenges facing our customer?
   b. How did we address those challenges?
   c. What were the results?
   d. What did the customer tell us were the benefits of those results?

e. Can we use any of the names attached to these stories?

- Again, using those same success stories as a reference point, list:
  a. What were the features each of those current customers purchased; and
  b. What were the benefits those customers derived from those features?
- Combine our answers and rank them in the order that we believe customers buy from us.
- Apply it as follows:
  "The reason I was specifically calling you today was that our customers have had a lot of success *(insert most powerful approach above)* and I'd like to stop by your office and share with you how they were able to accomplish that."

If you'd like to read a more robust article about how to write powerful cold call value propositions, go to our website at www.caponipg.com, find the articles archive and look for the article entitled *Three Simple Steps to Create a Powerful Cold Calling Value Proposition.*

6. *Assume that we can help them do what they are currently doing—better than they are currently doing it.*

"I can save you money over what you're paying today!" "I can make you more productive and save you time!" Ever had someone call you with a message like these? If it's not in the opening message, a lot of cold callers resort to this approach as we try to talk the person we're calling into meeting with us. When I hear that, I get even more upset at the interruption than I was when I realized that it was a cold call.

We lose credibility when we make those types of statements because it assumes that we have intimate knowledge of their current situation—and in most cases we don't. (This does assume we haven't done our homework and do know that we can help them. If we did though, the message would still be slightly different—but that's a topic for another day.)

How do we know what they're paying or how well they're doing? For that matter, how do we even know they use what we're selling? We *do* want to find out if we can help them, but let's not use the assumptive position that we can. It's insulting and makes us sound like the proverbial telemarketer.

One last thought. Go ahead and use this approach if you've been able to help 100 percent of the prospects you entered into a buying cycle with—because you're selling the proverbial better mousetrap. Take advantage of it while you can. It won't last long.

7. *Not internalizing our message.*

One of the biggest reasons I hear sales professionals use when they say they don't want to cold call is that they don't want to sound like the proverbial telemarketer. They complain that those callers just seem to be reading their scripts in a monotone voice.

Actually, I couldn't agree more. That occurs when we don't take ownership of our message and internalize it until we sound conversational. If we're reading a script, we *do* sound like the proverbial telemarketer.

Only 7 percent of effective communications is derived through the words we use. The biggest percentage of effective communications on a phone call comes from tonality (38 percent). Therefore we must not only *own* our message, we must deliver it with passion. There is only one way that the passion can come through—and that's if we know what we're going to say so we can concentrate on how we deliver it.

You do believe in what you sell, don't you? Well then, know what you're going to say and deliver it with passion.

8. *Winging it on each call.*

Above, we talked about how not to sound like we're reading our script by internalizing our message. The other alternative is to wing it on each call so that our message is different each time.

The problem with *winging it* is that if we deliver a different message each time, we can't predict and control the responses we'll get. That makes the task of handling those negative responses even more difficult.

Remember, that if we deliver the same message each time, we'll get the same few negative responses each time. Getting the same negative responses each time reduces the number of counters that we've got to learn and practice.

Don't fall into the trap of thinking that winging it is the easy way out. It's not. It's one of the things that make cold calling feel so difficult.

9. *Asking leading questions.*

This is an example of one of my favorites I hear from time to time, "You would like to save money wouldn't you?" Remember that less than 5 percent of the people we call think that they are in the market for what we're selling when we call. If they don't think they need us and don't want to talk to us, this kind of question just backs them into a corner (How can they answer no to that question without sounding like an idiot?). It is offensive, and does nothing but tick them off even more at the interruption, making the call even more confrontational.

10. *Not leaving voice mails—or leaving long-winded ones.*

The advertising industry says that it takes seven to ten touches for someone to even remember our name, let alone our value proposition, so why waste the effort involved in making the call and not leave a message?

Think of it as personal advertising. So what if they don't return this particular call? They don't always call when they see one of our ads, do they? And what better way to leave a message that should mean something to this particular target? It's better than advertising!

If that's not enough of a reason for you, think about this. When we make a call to someone, most of the time investment has already been spent. You've had to review your list of targets to call, determine who will be called, determine where you are in the process with this particular target, dial the phone, get through the phone tree, etc. Our benchmarks indicate that, at this point, we've already invested a minimum of four or five minutes without the right automation, and 1.5 to 2.5 minutes with the right automation (see below). So what's another twenty to thirty seconds? (Your messages shouldn't be any longer than that anyway.)

In order to craft well thought out, concise voice mails, go back to how to create our best value propositions as laid out in Rule No. 2 and use those. Each time we call during a cycle, we recommend leaving a different message. And if you've got the automation to do it efficiently (we recommend a product called Klpz from Contact Science), send a coordinated e-mail to double the number of *touches* in each attempt.

11. *When leaving voice mails, not saying our phone number s-l-o-w-l-y and repeating it.*

As Andy Rooney might whine, "Have you ever gotten a voice mail with a telephone number left so fast that you had to listen to it multiple times before you got the whole number?" Well, I have and I know that you have because it is all too common.

You know what I do with those voice mails? If I can't get the number after the second attempt, I delete it. And, heck, I think every cold call to me is a prospect, so I've got an incentive to listen. Trust me—the rest of the world is not so kind.

In our Prospector's Academies on **The Formula**, we actually role-play leaving voice mails. What we hear a lot in those role-plays is nervousness. That nervousness generally represents itself in speed. Slow down a little bit. If you think that your voice mail is too long, then it is. Work on shortening it, but make sure you leave your number twice and say it s-l-o-w-l-y.

By the way, if you think that you needn't repeat it because you're leaving it from a landline to a landline, think about how often we retrieve our office voice mails with our cell phones? Ever had one of those clicks happen that seems to cover up a word or number? That causes us to have to listen to the whole message again, right? Make it easy on our targets to do business with us! Leave your number twice and say it s-l-o-w-l-y.

12. *Not letting the target know when this will be the last.*

Many participants in **The Formula's** Prospector's Academies say that no one returns voice mails anyway, so why bother leaving them? Well, here's the biggest reason of them all to do so!

Our methodology includes the practice of leaving voice mails—and we've talked about the many advantages of doing so in these blogs in the past, so I won't repeat them all here. But think about this for a moment.

We've invested (hopefully) a lot of time developing the value propositions that we want our targets to hear regarding why they should meet with us. Why? Because we know that there are people out there that *are* in the market for what we sell when we call. So we know that we'll hit targets that do want to talk with us from time to time, right?

One of the two ground rules of cold calling, though, is that we are interrupting people when we call them, which means we must acknowledge that they're busy doing something when we call—even if they happen to be in the market for our solution. If we do not inform them that this is the last time we will call for a while, they may not call us back assuming (incorrectly) that we'll try again later.

Disciples of **The Formula** consistently report back that they get more returned voice mails off of this move-on message than any other.

To implement this technique, the first thing we need to do is determine how many attempts we'll make to reach a target prior to moving on to another. (We call that a cycle.) When we get to the last call, try something like this:

"Good morning, Mark. My name is Barry Caponi, and I'm the president of the Caponi Performance Group. As you know, I've left you several messages over the past few weeks, and although I'm persistent, I certainly don't want to be a pest. If you've been as busy as most of my customers are, but meaning to return my call, please do so since I'm looking forward to talking with you. If you can't, I won't bother you again right now, but will call you back again in a few months if you don't mind. My number is (817) 224-9900—that's (817) 224-9900. Thanks and I look forward to hearing from you."

You'll be pleased with the result when implementing this technique!

13. *Calling the same day and/or time of day over and over again, or calling the same person over and over again the same day.*

Albert Einstein once said that the definition of insanity is "doing the same thing over and over, but expecting different results."

One of the basic tenets behind *The Formula* is having a plan (we call them Best Practices) and then employing technology (we use a specialized tool called Klpz that works as a front end to CRMs —www.contactscience. com) to track what you do so that we can better leverage what works and change what doesn't.

Every industry and target group has windows that are better than others are for contacting them. The challenge is to figure out what works best for them and for us. I've heard sales professionals say that they make a hundred dials a day! Remember that the devil is in the detail.

Activity—or working hard—alone will not dictate success. It is not until we take a look at the individual elements of a calling plan (Best Practice) that we are able to begin to improve our performance. Are we only calling ten different people ten times per day? Are we always calling between eight and nine o'clock in the morning? Are we always calling on Monday?

In order to improve our performance, we must monitor what we do, measure what we do, and manage (or change) what we do.

If you call the same target multiple times per day and don't leave voice mails, you might also want to think about this for a second. In this world of caller ID, do you really think that your targets don't know you're a cold caller when your number shows up on their caller ID multiple times during the day? Remember that more and more people are using voice mail to screen.

What is the moral of this story? We need to think about what we do and why we do it. Then monitor the activity, measure the results, and manage accordingly.

THERE'S ACTUALLY NO DIFFERENCE BETWEEN A COLD CALL AND A WARM CALL.

Contrary to popular belief, there really is no difference between what happens on a cold call versus a warm call.

In our Prospector's Academies, we constantly hear, "I don't cold call. I network and follow-up on marketing-generated leads." So what is the difference between a *cold* call and a *warm* call?

There are four components to an appointment-making call regardless of whether it is cold or warm. The acronym is ARCA.

1. The **A**pproach
2. The target's **R**esponse (No)
3. Our **C**ounter
4. Asking for the **A**ppointment again

On a warm call, the Approach will vary slightly because we want to invoke either the name of the person who suggested that we call or the fact that they had asked us to contact them through a marketing program of some kind. The process and techniques we use to enlist the help of a gatekeeper, leave a message, send a coordinated e-mail, gain their attention, introduce ourselves, etc., is the same on any of these warm calls or a cold call.

If we really think about it, the target's response is also generally the same as on a cold call. They're just nicer about it. A referral target may say, "Hey, I appreciate Barry suggesting you call, but we're all set in that area." That's because in very few instances does the referrer know the target's business in enough detail to know they need us, can afford us, and that the timing is right for the call.

Even in the case of an inbound request for information from a lead-program, we sometimes are surprised by a negative response to a request for an appointment. However, it's not uncommon for an inbound request to be a tire-kicker or information-gatherer and not someone that's *in the Market* right now for what we are selling. Maybe they just want us to *send something*. Certainly this does not happen all the time, but it happens more than we think.

There are also many times that a different challenge occurs on these calls—the temptation to *sell* on the appointment-making call because of their interest. So how do we keep from falling prey to this? Easy—we use the same process we do on a cold call to provide only enough value to get the appointment.

The reason that our curriculum is called ***The Formula*** even though we talk a lot about cold calling—is that the process or *formula* that we apply in a warm call also applies in a cold call. It's all appointment-setting—and we must be prepared in order to be successful.

THE VALUE OF KNOWING OUR METRICS.

What we don't know about our performance will hurt us.

If we don't know how to effectively take someone who does not believe they are *in the market* for what we are selling *when* we pick up the phone and call, we will have to make many more calls for each appointment we set than we need or want to—and most of us have limited time to invest in cold calling.

Our surveys consistently show that less than 5 percent of any universe of targets *believes* that they are in the market for what we're selling when we call. If we take our target's word for it, less than five out of every hundred people we *talk to* should have an interest in meeting with us when we call. Our experience and calling metrics teach us that we'll not be able to convince all of those to meet with us for a variety of reasons, but let's assume for the sake of argument that we can.

Assumptions:

- Average time per dial = 6 minutes without Klpz, 3 minutes with it (includes prep time, calling, conversing, and recording the results)—trust me, we've documented it
- Typical Conversation Ratio = 10 percent (Dial to Conversations)
- Typical Appointment Ratio = 20 percent (Conversations to Appointments)
- Closing Ratio = 20 percent (Initial Meeting to Close)
- Percent *in the market* = 5 percent

Based on these averages, if we dial the phone a thousand times, we'll get through to fifty people. Of those fifty conversations, we'll only run into 2.5 that are in the market for what we're selling right now. Even assuming that they're all willing to meet with us, we've now invested six thousand minutes (one hundred hours) to get those appointments. So how much does our average sales professional make an hour? Is it worth it just to play the numbers game—or should we be learning how to convince some of those people that we've got something that others in their position have benefitted from? You do the math...

CHAPTER 2:
THE SCIENCE OF APPOINTMENT MAKING

Science is all about process and efficiency, as being effective alone is not enough. It is about staying organized, being in it for the long run, and being able to determine what's working and what's not. These aspects are all critical to our success.

The Science component of the ColdCalling101™ solution is based on Klpz, from Contact Science (see www.contactscience.com). It is a specialized web-based telephone prospecting management application that delivers measurable efficiency improvements. Klpz enables sales professionals to confidently execute their designed Best Practices in the most efficient way possible. With the support of Klpz, sales professionals efficiently spend just the right amount of time on each step of their Best Practice process:

- Consistently be able to accomplish tasks more accurately;
- Deliver results with less physical and mental effort;
- Benefit from automated tracking and reporting of results; and
- Confidently handle hundreds of targets simultaneously.

EFFECTIVENESS VERSUS EFFICIENCY IN THE APPOINTMENT-SETTING PROCESS.

What's the difference and why should I care?

Increasing our effectiveness is obviously important to our selling efforts as why would one want to make any more appointment-setting calls than necessary. However, realizing that there are only a certain number of hours in our selling day, doing what we must do as efficiently as possible is just as important, yet is seldom addressed.

I am a sales consultant and trainer by trade. Before I came to recognize the importance of both effectiveness and efficiency I traditionally focused on just helping sales professionals become more effective at their craft. For instance, if I could help sales professionals get through to the decision maker more often and turn more of those discussions into appointments, I felt I had done my job.

However, no matter how effective that sales professional gets at setting appointments, they will still have to invest that same amount of time per dial in the process of making those dials.

Over the years, companies have invested much time and money in tools that make the overall selling process more efficient. Sales force automation and customer relationship management software are two very important tools in that battle. However, for the person who must set first appointments (Initial Appointments) with new targets, those tools do not cut the mustard. They were not designed to be of benefit until the target becomes a prospect.

I use and recommend a tool called Klpz that was designed to make appointment-making more efficient. I have lowered my average time per dial from approximately six minutes to less than three minutes. That provides me the ability to either make twice the number of dials in the same amount of time, or make the same number of dials in half the time.

If I remain just as effective (and I am *very* effective on the phone, by the way) as I was before using Klpz, and I choose to invest the same amount of time making calls, I will *double* my sales if all other things remain equal.

PRIORITIES AND THE NEED TO SET APPOINTMENTS.

How to get our sales professionals to make those appointment-making calls each week.

During our Coldcalling101 Prospector's Academies, we always see a very substantial (double or better) increase in the number of dials being made, conversations with decision makers had, and of course, Initial Appointments being set. When Klpz is implemented, we also see that once the academy is over and we are gone, the number of dials has the tendency to drop back off to a reduced level. Why does that happen?

We believe it is all a matter of priorities on the part of the sales professional, and just as importantly, the sales manager. As I said in my white paper, *Is Cold Calling Really Dead? Searching for the elusive 'Silver Bullet'*, "There is no better way to proactively control our own destiny than to make more effective appointment-making calls. There is a direct correlation between the number of dials made and the size of one's commission."

What we believe happens is that during the academy, making dials is the priority. It is scheduled into the program and is a main focus during the review sessions. As soon as the academy is over and the focus shifts to closing those Initial Appointments that became prospects, we tend to go back to old habits—fit in the dials when we have time, or only when we think we need to make them. (There is also the issue that the pipeline is fuller for the first time in a while, draining time away from setting appointments with new targets. One could make the argument that this is the penalty for successfully setting so many appointments!)

The reduction in dials has two impacts though:

1. We get less practice with the new techniques which means those new skills can atrophy because they are not yet second nature (it takes twenty-one days to establish a new habit according to Stephen Covey); and

2. Fewer dials mean fewer Initial Appointments after the pipeline is exhausted again. Going back to the phone is tougher to do than continuing to do it.

Whether you are in one of our programs or not, there is a lesson to be learned here. As managers, we must *insist* that each sales professional make appointments with *themselves* on their calendar each week to make the appropriate number of dials. This should *consistently* be done prior to any other appointments being set.

HOW MANY INITIAL APPOINTMENTS DO WE NEED?

Why is it important to know that?

It is important to know how many Initial Appointments we need each year, month, and week, in order to make our annual goal. Why? It is the easiest activity based goal that can be monitored, measured and managed on a weekly and even daily, basis. If we don't have enough Initial Appointments on our calendar for next week, we know we need to get on the phone and fix it today before we get too far behind the proverbial *8 Ball*.

We suggest that this is one of the most important questions we have to answer each year and it takes four quick steps to calculate it.

1. First, take the revenue that must come from new customer sales this year and divide it by the average size of those sales. That will give us the number of new sales we will need.

2. Next, we need to estimate our Close Ratio. We do that by measuring the sales we make divided by the number of Initial Appointments we need to go on in order to close those new sales.

3. Now, take the number of new sales needed (answer from question number 1) and divide it by the Close Ratio we got from answering question number 2. That will give us the number of actual Initial Appointments we need to go on this year.

4. Lastly, we'll take that number and divide it by the number of *full* selling weeks we have available to us this year (44 in most cases).

For example, if my goal of $240,000 is divided by an average size sale of $12,000 (Step 1), it equals twenty new customers. When twenty is multiplied by the 25 percent Close Ratio (Step 2), the result of that calculation shows that I need eighty Initial Appointments. If there are forty-four full selling weeks in a year (typical selling calendar believe it or not), I need to average two per week (actually 1.8 to be precise).

It's much easier to manage to that number than to keep looking at that $240,000 quota and wonder where it will come from.

HOW TO RID OURSELVES OF THOSE DREADED DRY SPELLS.

Almost all of us from time to time have a great month or quarter with great closing numbers followed by a miserable month or quarter with nothing to show for our efforts. There is a way to reduce the risk of that occurrence.

Figure out:

1. How many Initial Appointments we need to hit our required sales goal during the year.

2. How many discussions we need in order to generate those Initial Appointments.

3. How many times we'll need to dial the phone in order to get the requisite number of discussions with the targets we'd like to meet with.

4. Divide that number by two hundred-twenty (the typical number of selling days in the year) and we have the number of dials needed to make each day.

5. How much time does it take to accomplish a dial in the appointment-making process? That, by the way, includes figuring out who to call, where are we in the pursuit of this that particular target, what we're going to say, dialing the phone number, saying what we want to (when successful getting through), leaving messages when we don't, sending e-mail follow ups, and recording the results of the attempt. Without the right tool, our benchmarks indicate it will take about six minutes on average. With Klpz (the tool I recommend), we can literally cut that in half.

6. To determine the amount of time necessary to make the calls, multiply the number of calls needed per day times the average time per call shown in (Step 5) above and you've got the number of minutes you'll need each day to hit your number.

Once we have the answers to those questions, we know how much time we'll need each week to keep a steady stream of targets coming in the top of our funnel. We must set aside the time on our calendars to make those calls first, and then make that time sacrosanct. If a target or a prospect says that they want to meet us during one of those periods we have designated on our calendar for calling, say no and suggest another time. People respect those that are busy and will find another agreeable time that works for both of us.

There is no better way to control our own destiny than to make more effective appointment-making calls as there is a direct correlation between the number of dials attempted and sales made.

COLD CALLING IS MORE THAN ABOUT JUST MAKING DIALS.

The appointment-making process is not just the numbers game *that most of us sales managers believe it is.*

"Make enough dials and you'll get sales!" we tell our teams. And when our charges aren't setting enough Initial Appointments, we respond with another platitude, "Make more dials!" Let me explain why this is a dangerous thought through a story.

A colleague of mine, Stu Schlackman (http://www.competitive-excellence.com) related the following story to me. When he was a young pup, he was hired by a sales training company, handed the yellow pages and told to get on the phone. In his first week, he literally made 1,000 dials (how many of us could do that)? He left six hundred-fifty voice mails, had fifty conversations of which forty-nine said no, so he hung up and moved on to the next name on the list. He said he got one appointment which closed (to an existing customer who told him they were going to call and buy again anyway).

What if he would have had a set of proven Best Practices and a process to follow? What if he would have known how to *counter* those forty-nine, "No," responses he heard? How about if he had had good voice mail scripts so that at least some of the six hundred-fifty voice mails would have returned his calls? What if he would have had good solid questions to ask (we call them *Bridge Questions*™[1]) that would have gotten his targets to stop thinking about how to get him off the phone for a moment and enter into a meaningful conversation where

---

1   See free white paper called ***The Appointment Making Formula*™** *Four Steps to More Effective Appointment-setting* at www.caponipg.com for a full description.

he could apply his considerable selling skills? And lastly, what if he had been able to make those thousand dials in half the time?

He didn't last very long there. And, by the way, who do you think the sales professional that followed him called? Probably started right at the front of the same yellow pages and called the same people, with management expecting the results to be different.

Now think about the time and money that was wasted recruiting him, vetting him, training him on what he was selling, and finally, paying him to make those calls. We have the tendency to think that our time is not *real* money. We're there anyway, so it doesn't *cost* any money out of pocket to repeat this process over and over, right?

Our company, the Caponi Performance Group, Inc., must also rely on the cold call, but our sales team would have had fifty-five Initial Appointments out of that thousand dials, and done it in half the time. Plus, using the tool we recommend, I would have had real time visibility into his results, so I could have taken corrective steps before Stu burned himself out and quit.

The appointment-setting process is not without cost. As a matter of fact, because it can be so demoralizing, it can be a very expensive one in many ways, even if your sales team is commission only.

ARE WE HOOKED ON HOPIUM WHEN IT COMES TO OUR TEAM'S ABILITY TO SET APPOINTMENTS?

Six Questions to ask ourselves to determine whether our team needs some help.

It's no secret that how well our team sets appointments to begin a new selling process has a direct impact on the new business revenue stream. Where their ability to set appointments with *new targets* can sometimes be masked is where sales professionals have responsibility to sell into existing accounts as well. The *new customer* Initial Appointments are mixed in with the calls into existing accounts. Additionally, most of us at a team level are measured on revenue and not on the acquisition of new customers, so we're not even that concerned about it as long as the revenue keeps rolling in. But those of us who have responsibility for building the business for the long term know that new customers are the lifeblood of any organization.

If the acquisition of new customers (and the process to get in front of new potential customers) is such a critical piece to the selling process, then why can't most sales managers we talk to articulate what their sales professionals are saying on the phone to set those appointments? They view the steps between dialing the phone and getting the appointment as another example of the proverbial *black box*. They have no idea how their team is actually performing on the calls.

Here's a way to test whether they need help or not. Have each of your team call *you* on the phone to ask for an appointment just as they would a target and then ask yourself the following questions:

1. If you weren't there, what kind of voice mail did they leave?

2. What was their value proposition? Was it consistent across your team or was each one *winging it*?

3. Did they sound confident and like they believed in what they were selling?

4. Did they talk about what they had done for others to generate interest or did they talk about what they could potentially do for you? (Remember, more than 95 percent of the targets our teams are calling don't believe they are in the market for our solution when we call—ergo, what we can do for them falls on deaf ears until we can get them into an open minded discussion.)

5. Was it all them talking or did they engage you?

6. When you said, "No thanks," were they able to consistently handle that negative response, and at least get into a

conversation that gave them another opportunity to ask for the appointment, or did they just give up?

EIGHT SIMPLE IDEAS TO HELP SALES MANAGEMENT FIX AN EMPTY PIPELINE.

Empty pipelines are brought on by a lack of prospecting activity. So how do we fix that on an ongoing basis?

First, an observation: If we know we're not setting enough Initial Appointments to feed that hungry beast, the pipeline, there is good news afoot! The fact that we even recognize that means we at least have a minimal set of metrics or we wouldn't even know that we're headed towards disaster. As I have pointed out in the past, when appointment-making is necessary, consistency in making the dials does make a difference.

So if our charges just aren't making the dials, what can we do if our selling model requires that the sales professional set their own appointments? Here are eight ideas:

1. First things first: people are more apt to buy into a goal they help set. So, take each person through a Sales Activity & ROI Calculator[5] exercise to help determine what is the appropriate number of appointments (and dials) needed each day. Then get them to commit to that number in writing. If that alone doesn't work, try these:

2. Have them show you each week where they've set aside the necessary Call Blocks on their calendars to make those calls.

3. If that doesn't work, have them come into the office and make those calls during their chosen Call Blocks.

4. If *that* doesn't work, then have *mandatory* Call Blocks in the office at times of your choosing. This can be done in a couple of ways.

    a. One of our customers uses what he calls Touch Point Tuesdays—no one leaves the office until the appointed number of Initial Appointments is set for the coming week.

    b. Set aside a specific time each day for calling until the appointed number of Initial Appointments is set for the coming week.

5. There is also a different approach that I've seen managers use effectively in managing remote sales professionals. Schedule a couple of days to go on calls with them in their territory and give them a minimum number of Initial Appointments and follow-up appointments you want to go on while you're there. If they don't set enough, tell them you're still coming. It will be embarrassing to say the least, not to mention that they'll have to sit there and make the dials in front of you during the times there aren't appointments set.

6. True call reluctance does exist and comes in a couple of different flavors

    a. First is a lack of process and skills, so that when the sales professional does make the calls, they are disillusioned by the process and results: "Boss, cold calling doesn't work. And besides, it's painful." ColdCalling101 can help you fix that.

    b. There can many times be a more fundamental and psychological block keeping them from picking up the phone. So when we see a sales professional worth saving, we work with a company (www.productivitycubed.com) that will work one-on-one with sales professionals to unblock the underlying causes. They guarantee their results by the way and are quite effective. See the resources page of our website for contact information.

7.   Get someone else to set the appointments for them. Check our website for a list of appointment-setting services that use our recommended tools, processes and skills;

8.   Lastly, well, you know what to do...

TRACKING RESULTS, COACHING AND COLD CALLING ACTIVITY.

Why is having our sales professionals just "make more dials" when their activity isn't generating enough new appointments actually counter-productive?

First, it is discouraging when the dials are being made with little to show for it. At best, it's a waste of time and at worst, it can cause turnover on the sales team. Secondly, it takes more time away from servicing customers and pipeline selling activities. So what to do, you ask?

If the team lives and dies by finding new business each month and must set new appointments with each prospect or target to do so, efficiency is a must. Keeping a few targets a month straight can be done in a spreadsheet or in a CRM. But if there are more than 10 names per week to be called, I submit that we must have a tool that is designed for this task.

I have personally tried the paper system (lots of folders), ACT! (I invested a lot of money optimizing it), an internally developed CRM, commercially available CRMs and Excel spreadsheets. In each case, I could not find enough time to keep track of everything that is necessary in order to continuously call a set of targets. Each time, with each tool, I became hopelessly lost, forgetting who I was pursuing, what progress I had made, and fell further and further behind in the process of documenting activity to the point that I gave up.

We suggest a tool called Klpz, from Contact Science, LLC, which was developed specifically for this task. Benchmarks show a minimum of a two to one improvement in the number of targets that can be pursued in an organized manner in a given amount of time. This makes a huge difference on a number of levels.

Here's an example from one of the many benchmarks we've run. Prospecting ten targets in a row using SalesForce.com took forty-eight minutes. Klpz took eighteen minutes. Unfortunately, most sales managers bought Sales Force thinking it could be used for this purpose (in addition to the things it *is* good at).

I know this sounds like heresy, but it's very true. Refusing to examine this can have catastrophic consequences.

One of the ancillary benefits of Klpz is that it provides accurate and granular reports as to where the team is failing. That, at least, will give you a place to start to examine how to fix the specific challenges you've got with each individual sales professional.

FIVE SIMPLE RULES TO KEEP CALLING ACTIVITY LEVELS CONSISTENT.

Consistency is more important than quantity when appointment-setting.

It is hard to stay consistent in the number of appointment-making calls we make over a month or year. What can we do to make it easier to accomplish?

We've talked before about how each of us has experienced one month or quarter that was an award winner almost always followed by a dud. We've also talked about knowing how many dials we need to make each week in order to hit our financial goals. Here are five simple rules to help eliminate the ups and downs of a weak pipeline.

1. Know how many dials are needed in a year (use our Sales Activity & ROI Calculator you can find on our website).

2. Periodically review how many dials we actually made during the last 90 days. When viewed against our plan, was it enough? Do we need to change the objective?

3. Once we've established an objective, commit to it. Write it down.

4. Set the time aside in each week on the calendar as an appointment with ourselves before setting any other calendar events.

5. Lastly, if our goal is let's say, ten dials a day, and we get busy and can't (or won't) get it done. Make five calls today. If we can't do that, make two. Get in the habit of making some dials every day. It will even out the ups and downs of the pipeline.

MAKING SOME MINIMUM OF COLD CALLING DIALS EACH DAY ADDS UP OVER THE YEAR.

In the previous blog, we talked about the power of consistency in our dialing habits. In this blog, we're going to offer a simple example to reinforce the value of making some dials each and every day.

We tend to fixate on today's goal—whether it is fifty dials or five. The easy way to justify not doing it today is to tell oneself, let's say, that it is only .5 percent of my year's total for instance (five dials per day times two hundred-twenty selling days per year). It's the approach most of us use every day. "No big deal, it's only five of eleven hundred I committed to make this year."

Next time that happens, try thinking about it in this way. If I make just two more dials today than I would have if I acquiesce and make none, what impact would that have on my success at the end of the year?

• Two dials times two hundred-twenty selling days in the year equals four hundred-forty dials over the year.

- If I get through to the decision maker 20 percent of the time and convert 25 percent of those conversations into appointments, I'll have twenty-two more Initial Appointments over a year's time.
- If I close 18 percent of those Initial Appointments, I'll have four more sales from just those two dials per day.
- So what is your average sized sale and more importantly, commission?

Do the math and start getting in the habit of making some calls every day.

THE VALUE OF CALL BLOCKS—MAKING A BUNCH OF CALLS TOGETHER.

We recommend that cold calls be done in a planned manner and in blocks of time.

We've said before that we should schedule time on our calendars to make calls each week before we put any other controllable dates on our calendars. Here's why.

1. If we try to *fit them in* between other things, they never get done, and if we're honest with ourselves, we know it.

2. Once into a Call Block, we get smoother and more comfortable with every call. Once on a roll, our effectiveness goes up. So schedule a long enough Call Block to allow that to happen. We suggest forty-five minutes to an hour. If we do choose to call longer than an hour at a time, we suggest taking a break so we don't start sounding rote.

3. If we're having success in a Call Block, do keep calling. It's fun and exciting when that happens, so take advantage of it.

4. If we're taking the *collar* as they say in baseball (zero for all attempts), take a break for a few minutes. Get away from the phone and do something else for a few minutes. *But*, we've still got to make the calls. It's all about the law of averages. Some Call Blocks are better than others and I have no idea why!

HOW CAN WE ASSURE THAT WE HAVE THE TIME TO MAKE CALLS?

Making our calling time sacrosanct.

The first appointments we should place on our calendar each week should be for the time we need to set aside for setting of appointments.

The Random House Dictionary of English Usage defines sacrosanct as, "extremely sacred or inviolable."Couldn't have said it better myself.

The sales process starts with getting our self in front of a target, doesn't it? Oh, we may quibble and say it starts with lead generation, but let's define that as a marketing function and get on with the discussion.

What is the most common complaint made by sales managers in pipeline review sessions? It's, "We need more activity," or "We're just not getting in front of enough people." As a sales trainer and consultant, I hear it all the time. I also hear, "Once we're in front of a target, we can sell." I'm not sure I agree with that in every case, but that's a topic for another day.

What they're really saying is that we're not doing enough appointment-setting. We gravitate to the activities that are more enjoyable and are necessary to shepherd that prospect through the buying cycle itself. We'll all do the fact finding, the proposals, and the closing presentations before we'll get back on the phone to set an Initial Appointment with another new target. Do it myself all too often. The result is the peaks and valleys of sales. We fill the front end of the sales funnel with Initial Appointments only when we have no more prospects left to sell. Then depending on the length of our buying cycles, we can pretty well predict how long our dry spell will last.

So how should we fix that? Set aside the time each week or day to make those calls and don't give up that time for anything. If a target, prospect, or even customer says they'd like to meet with us during one of those periods, to borrow an old phrase, "Just say no." Trust me, people respect the fact that we're busy and will agree to meet with us at another time. And yes, that even includes targets.

WHY GOALS ARE IMPORTANT IN COLD CALLING PROGRAMS.

I was swimming laps this morning and faced a dilemma. For some reason I did not have the energy I normally have, so early on in the workout I began to rationalize cutting the workout short. After all, I had worked out every morning this week so far, so why not *reward* myself—not to mention the fact that working out is not my favorite thing to do each day. (I do, however, like the results!)

I swam my whole workout plus a little extra, and felt even better about myself afterwards than if I had cut it short with my rationalization. Here's why you should care.

The reason I kept swimming is because I have a measureable goal of sixty laps per workout. I also was able to conjure some of those old coach's adages from my youth like, "Winners never quit," and "No pain no gain." I'm sure you've got a few more you could add to the list.

I kept swimming though, because I wanted to hit my goal for the day. In cold calling, it works the same way. It is also not one of my favorite things to do. I have a measureable goal and when I get close to that goal, I seem to get energized because I am accomplishing one of my goals.

Try it. Perhaps it'll work for you, too!

THE VALUE OF MAKING JUST ONE MORE DIAL IN A CALL BLOCK.

When I get close to the end of a Call Block, I get fired up! I know I must do this task, yet I don't necessarily like doing it. But once started, I get on a roll. As I get near the end, as I have mentioned before, I feel better about myself and I'm even more effective because my confidence soars. And when I hit my number and get to the end, unless I've got a time issue, I make *one more dial!*

If you think it doesn't make much of a difference, let's do the math based on the following assumptions:

1. Two hundred twenty selling days in the year;

2. Our average Conversation Ratio for the past year has been 18 percent (the percentage of dials that get through to the person I want to meet with);

3. Our average Appointment Ratio is 30 percent (the percentage of those conversations that become appointments);

4. Our Closing Ratio (as measured from the Initial Appointment) is 33 percent.

If I make just one more dial per day, I'll make two hundred twenty more by year's end. Applying our assumptions from above, I'll also have twelve more appointments during the year. Apply our Closing Ratio and average sized sale, and I'm looking at over $150,000 more in sales. "And that ain't hay," as they say!

WHY THE DRIVE BY SHOOTING APPROACH TO PROSPECTING IS COUNTERPRODUCTIVE.

The *Rule of 45* says that 45 percent of sales leads will turn into sales in the next twelve months, and that 75 percent intend to purchase at some point. The catch is that it may not necessarily be us that will get the sale.

Great sales professionals keep calling until the target *buys or dies* as the old saying goes. If a lead is several months old, there is still an 80 percent chance that the target has yet to make a purchase.

One last thought; the older the lead, the less likely our competitors are following through on them either. Let them be the ones that give up, not us.

From one point of view, it's actually counterproductive to give up too soon. The reason for that is that we had to invest time to try the few times we did originally, right? That now represents sunk costs, as the accountants call it. By going on to yet another target and following the same unproductive pattern (of giving up too soon), we'll never recoup those sunk costs.

The important point of the story though is how, not if, we're going to follow up. The operative challenge is how to stay organized so we don't forget to call on targets efficiently and effectively over time according to a well thought out process. Without one, it's no wonder why 88 percent of all leads are never followed up on thoroughly.

Coldcalling101 users don't even have to worry about it as our tool (Klpz) is the epitome of the *set and forget* approach to following up on a target.

Build that well thought out process (we call them Best Practices) and Klpz won't let us forget.

IS YOUR SALES TEAM JUST GOING THROUGH THE MOTIONS WHEN MAKING COLD CALLS?

Or are all of those calls resulting in new business?

I received a call from one of our new customers this week. He was very excited because for the first time he could see exactly what his teams were doing in terms of cold calling. He's a regional sales manager with several sales teams that were trained before the first of the year through one of our appointment-setting Prospectors Academies™.

He told us that his sales professionals had been truly pounding the phones now for a couple of months since the training which fixed his lack of activity problem. He also said that the activity was very consistent across his districts. He was also pleased with the fact he was now able to start deep drilling on the process and results a bit more instead of just focusing on the activity levels as he had been doing in the past.

Reading his weekly Klpz reports had gotten him to ask why some of his guys were setting appointments like crazy and some were not, though. As a matter of fact, he was able to see that the ones that were being successful were all in the same districts. He told us that when he role-played with the different districts though, they sounded pretty much the same. He told us that the teams that were not setting the appointments were getting discouraged and so were their managers. Here's a synopsis of what we found:

- We ran a report that found that his districts that were not performing differed in one key area from those that were having success. To put it frankly, their lists were awful. The successful districts were seeing about a 35 percent removal rate of names when going through a new list and the unsuccessful ones were seeing more than 80 percent of the names removed.

What this means is that after following the four steps in the process of contact we set up (we call them Cycles), the sales professional has three choices of what to do with the target: recycle them for one hundred twenty days and try again; declare Success (they met with them and began a Buying Cycle); or Remove them from the list. After speaking with the District Managers, it became clear that the managers that had taken the time to put some effort into better qualifying and defining the lists their charges would call into, were experiencing the most success. The ones that did not were filled with targets that were not good fits. For instance, many of the targets were too small.

There are two morals to the story. First is that by adding what we call *Science*, or Klpz, to the challenge of prospecting for new customers, the managers gained access to valuable information none of us have ever had access to before to help improve the prospecting processes.

Second, we've talked about the value of investing time in refining lists and building territories over time in this blog before, so we know the importance of this.

And by the way, just imagine the potential consequences of what might have happened if he hadn't been able to define the problem. Would have some of his sales professionals quit because of the frustration? Would he have incorrectly assumed he had a closing problem or a sales professional problem instead of a list problem?

THE FOUR ELEMENTS OF THE APPOINTMENT-SETTING PROCESS WE CAN IMPROVE.

What are they and how do we improve them?

A lot of us are what we like to call, *Hooked on Hopium,* when it comes to the success of our prospect acquisition strategy. Many of us concentrate most of our energy and focus on pursuing prospects that are already in the pipeline. After all, that's how we get paid, right? We don't get commissions for finding prospects; we get paid to close them. Our teams are good at closing, but suck (technical selling term) at consistently filling the pipeline with quality prospects.

This is a four part blog that focuses on the four main elements of a prospect acquisition process and how to move the needle in a positive direction on each. The four parts are:

1. Target Acquisition (who we call)

2. Art Skills (what do we say, and how and when do we say it)

3. Best Practices (process and messaging)

4. Science Skills (efficiency and improvement)

Part 1 – Target Acquisition

This may be truly one of real *elephants in the room* issues. Every sales manager and sales professional thinks about this. The question is whether they really think it through or not.

We hear a very consistent message when talking to both these groups. Sales professionals just want to be handed a list of targets to be called. Sales managers want them to go find their own. As soon as the sales professional has a *list*, the sales manager is relieved and goes back to more *important* duties such as forecasting for the boss or trying to help someone close a deal. In other words, the objective incongruously seems to be the procurement of the list, not the ultimate goal of acquiring as many good new targets as we can so that our selling process is more effective and efficient.

Here's what we're missing and why it is so important. This may be the most critical component of the process of getting in front of prospective new customers. Why do I say that?

1. *Every* other step in the selling process stems from the success of this step. Each of us is given the same number of hours each year to accomplish our task of bringing home some amount of new revenue and new customers. If we invest that time wisely calling on a set of well qualified targets, we'll do well. Invest it poorly on a list of targets that are too small, outside our range of profitability, don't use our solution, etc. and we will fail unless we get lucky.

2. What good are great skills at getting through and converting conversations into appointments if our list doesn't contain targets that are of the right size for instance?

Not only do we waste time trying to set the appointments, but we also waste even more time once in front of the target qualifying them. And if our qualification skills are poor, we'll waste even more time trying to sell to them and service them after the sale.

3. What good did the time we invested to create a good set of the Best Practices do us if we cannot leverage our prospecting time each day by building our territory with targets that are truly qualified but may just not be *in the market* right now? A well thought out set of Best Practices applied to this concept will reduce the amount of cold calling we must do over time because these same targets remain on the list until they are in the market. I begin establishing credibility and, at least, a Dialogue Bond[6] each time I speak with them. However, if I constantly must start all over with a new list, I am doing neither.

What good does it do us to simply be efficient or fast at reaching out to the wrong targets? None. We're just failing faster.

The moral of the story is that, particularly as managers, we need to give great thought to, and invest the appropriate time in, helping our sales professionals acquire a good set of targets. We should ask ourselves what kind of lead generation programs are in play? How well are they working? Should we canvas? If we purchase lists, have we designed the criteria well enough?

Trust me—it will pay us back in spades, even if the current sales professionals can't cut the mustard. At least we're continuing to warm up the territory over time.

Part 2 – Art Skills

We just began asking participants who register for our webinars the question of which of these four categories of challenges pose the greatest challenge for them. The answer was overwhelmingly, number two: Art Skills. Most sales professionals just don't know what to say to open the conversation, let alone what to say when the target says, "No."

There's not a whole lot I can do to help fix this challenge in a single blog. However, I can help you identify whether it is something we, as managers, need to address. Here's what I would suggest:

1. Invest in Klpz as a process engine for telephone prospecting because it will (among other really neat things) automatically provide two key ratios to determine whether our charges are struggling with Art.
   a. The first ratio is the Conversation Ratio—how many dials does it take to produce a conversation with the decision maker our sales professional wishes to meet with. In addition to this being a list problem, a low ratio here suggests that we should test how well our charges are leaving voice mails, sending coordinated e-mails and how well they handle gatekeepers.
   b. The second ratio is the Appointment Ratio— how many conversations does it take to produce an appointment. A low ratio here has only one principle root cause—what they say, when they say it, and how they say it once they are speaking with the person with whom they wish to meet. The list could also contribute to a low ratio here, although it generally has manifested itself as a problem before getting to this point.
2. Okay, maybe number 1 is a bit self-serving, but it really does work. So let's try this if we're unwilling or unable to do step 1. Let's ask our charges to begin writing down the results of their appointment-setting process. If not using

Klpz, first have them record the time they begin and end making a Call Block. Then have them make a tick mark each time they:

  a. Dial the phone (D);
  b. Complete a conversation with the person they wish to meet with (CC);
  c. Leave a voice mail (LVM);
  d. Get a returned voice mail (RVM); and
  e. Schedule an Initial Appointment (IA)

Trust me, it won't be exactly accurate, but it will begin to paint a very valuable picture. We'll begin to see patterns and gain insight into the process we've not had before. For instance, we'll begin to see things like they are not making as many dials as they say they are because the time they say they are making calls doesn't match up with what we know they are doing with their days. (By the way, figure on at least 6 minutes a dial if they use a CRM or contact manager; more if they are using spreadsheets or hand written lists. We've benchmarked it.)

3. In the next sales meeting, ask the team what is the number one negative response they are hearing when they get the decision maker on the phone. Then role-play how they are handling it. And by the way, the lower the Appointment Ratio, the more we need to be prepared to cringe when we hear what they are saying.

4. In a subsequent sales meetings ask them to role-play:
  a. Leaving voice mails
  b. Handling gatekeepers

5. If feeling overwhelmed at the result–call us. Our typical customer will double or better the number of appointments their teams set.

Okay, sorry for the second commercial in this blog, but the point is if you will do at least steps 2 through 4, you'll have a really good idea of whether or not Art is something you need to address.

Part 3 – Best Practices

The concept of Best Practices contains a lot of different disciplines that apply to both Art (effectiveness) and Science (efficiency), but let me address at least a few key ones:

1. Are we managing our particular area of responsibility with the concept of territory management in mind? In other words, regardless of who is in a specific territory (virtual or geographic), are *we* employing a process that will leave the territory better defined and warmer a year from now regardless of whether our current sales professional is still here?

2. Do we have a Best Practice that defines the number of times a target will be called, how frequently, and if no contact is made, how long will we wait to begin the Cycle again?

3. Do we have our team professionally disengage at the end of a call, asking for permission to check back again in the future if the target is not *in the market* right now, or do they take the *no* they hear as a *never*?

4. Do we have our team leave voice mails? Are they different for each attempt in the Cycle? It is a great way to leave a commercial message if it is crafted well. And who knows, if the messages are different, sometimes we actually do hit on a hot button by varying our value proposition between several of our strongest.

5. Does the target know that the last attempt *is* the last attempt for a while? In other words, are we giving the

target a last chance to respond if they want to but were too busy to call back earlier?

6. How do we on-board new sales professionals? How do we provide them with the Best Practices that are working for our current team?

7. Can we tell within the first thirty to forty-five days whether our new team member has the aptitude and attitude to succeed or do we wait for the revenue attainment (or lack thereof) to tell us that several months down the road?

There are actually a lot more questions I could ask here that we step our customers through to determine how best to tackle this key part of the selling process, but any more at this time I'd either bore you or depress you!

Part 4 – Science

Science is all about speed, organization and reporting on the ability to pursue targets using the prescribed set of Best Practices.

Our Creator has given all of us the same number of hours each week to attain our goals. In the world of telephone prospecting that is usually stated in terms of the fact that each of us has only so many dials in us each year. How we expend those dials is directly proportional to our success. For instance, the product for this process I recommend, Klpz, was designed specifically for this task. Therefore, our benchmarks show (and our customers report) that a caller can easily double the number of dials being made per hour of calling. So if we can either increase the number of attempts being made without increasing the time commitment, or make the same number of attempts in half the time, should we not sell more?

Those that do take the time to design and institute a set of well thought out Best Practices generally would like for their charges to be able to follow those Best Practices accurately. Science is the way that is enforced.

How many times have we (or any of our charges) forgotten to call someone back when requested? Unless we are super heroes, the answer is probably fairly often, but absolutely occasionally. It's why organizations invest a lot of money in CRM applications, contact managers and the like thinking they will solve this problem.

Lastly, science helps us improve the process by measuring the results and doing so in a way that we are provided the necessary data in a meaningful way (information).

IF COLD CALLING, HOW MANY TARGETS CAN A SALES PROFESSIONAL PURSUE EACH YEAR?

How to design a Best Practice.

Why is that important to understand? Several reasons:

1. In other blogs, I shared some statistics that indicate that most appointments (and sales) are set/made on the fifth through the twelfth attempts, not on the first. Therefore, we should have a *Best Practice* that includes reaching out to qualified targets at least that many times, although not necessarily all at once.

2. There is also finite number of dials each of our sales professionals has to invest each year. For instance, if our sales professionals commit to calling one hour a day and leave voice mails, they can effectively make about twenty dials an hour if they use our recommended product, Klpz. Therefore, they only have the capacity to make forty-four hundred dials over a typical year (two hundred-twenty selling days). The operative question should then be how to best invest those forty-four hundred dials. "Waste not, want not," as the old saying goes.

3. Lastly, lead generation, list generation, and list purchase can be expensive. Sales professionals by nature tend to be impatient. They try to contact someone a couple of times, and if they aren't successful, they turnaround and ask, "May I have another please?"

   If we understand that it takes many attempts to get the appointment, it is wasteful to not have a Best Practice in place that contains rules for multiple attempts to reach someone. It is also doubly wasteful to throw a name away that has not been pursued adequately enough, as we not only wasted the investment in attempting to contact the first target, but we also then turn around and unnecessarily invest in the acquisition of another one to replace that one.

So now that I've made this suggestion that we should have a Best Practice for cold calling, you are probably asking:

1. What's involved in the design of one of these Best Practices?

2. Is there also a way to figure out how many targets a sales professional could reasonably pursue in a year?

Let's examine the components of a Best Practice, or framework, for what we call a Cycle. Here are some simple questions to ask ourselves when designing one. But before I do that, here's an example of a Cycle.

4 x 5 x 90

The first number designates the number of attempts I will make in this particular Cycle. The second number indicates the number of business days between calls and the third number tells us how many days we'll wait until we start a new Cycle assuming we do not reach the person during this Cycle.

There is no exact science to the design of appointment-setting Best Practices, but here are a few questions to ask ourselves when designing a Cycle:

1. What level of buyer am I calling into? The easier it is to get a hold of the person we're calling does have bearing on both the number of attempts and the delay between calls.

2. How many targets are there in my universe of potential targets? The more there are, the fewer attempts I might make during a Cycle. I might also want to increase the time I wait before attempting another round of calls, because I want to reach out to more targets each year. If I have a very few targets in my universe, I would probably at least shorten the wait between Cycles.

3. When do I cross the line between being a persistent sales professional and becoming a pest or irritant?

Let's tackle the topic of how to figure out how many targets is the *right* number for a particular sales professional or territory.

Take a look at the chart below. It comes from our Sales Activity & ROI Calculator[7]. The key fields are the number of minutes invested per day, steps (most likely telephone calls) per day, the number of times we'll actually go through a Cycle per year, and the estimate of how many targets will be replaced because they were unqualified or they became customers and are now on a different list. Reasonably, that number generally falls somewhere between seven hundred-fifty and twelve hundred; much more than that and we're into the *drive by shooting* approach of trying a few times and give up.

How many targets can you pursue a year?		
1-	Minutes per day on the phone	60
2-	Average number of steps taken in your Best Practice before a "pursuit" ends	3.5
3-	Average time per Step (CRMs are typically 6 minutes, Klpz is less than 3)	3.0
	Number of steps you can make a day	20.0
4-	Number of days per year you will telephone prospect	220
5-	Number of times a target will be "pursued" per year until you reach them	2.0
6-	Replacement targets, as percent of total, that are needed to keep your calling list at the right size	25%
	You need a list with this many names	786

Let me explain a few of these specific data points for you.

No. 2 refers to the number of attempts we normally have to make during a give Cycle before we get them. In this case, it takes between three and four attempts on average before we get them. This number can actually be taken right out of Klpz reports if you're using it. Otherwise, you'll have to estimate it.

No. 3 refers to the average duration of a call. This number can also be taken right out of a Klpz report. Otherwise, it also will also need to be estimated. (If you're not using Klpz and are looking for an estimate, use six minutes per attempt.)

No. 5 refers to how many Cycles will be performed per year in pursuing the typical targets on this list. The more limited our universe of targets, the more times we'll typically pursue them. If we are selling into a horizontal market with many, many targets, we may choose to touch more, so we'll reduce the number of times we'll conduct a Cycle on a target in a given year. (Every six months is about the minimum I'd recommend. Any less frequently than that and we lose the value of the cumulative attempts as our target will not remember us very well.)

No. 6 refers to the number of targets that will be thrown off the list either because we discover they were unqualified or they became a customer.

The point is simply this. By knowing the number of targets a sales professional or territory can support can help us when dividing up territories, setting quotas, and figuring budgets for acquiring target lists. Our customers tell this has been helpful information to have.

IS THE, "MAKE MORE DIALS!" MANTRA THE BEST WAY TO SET MORE COLD CALLING APPOINTMENTS?

Many customers we've worked with originally only had their sales teams reporting to management each week the number of dials they were making to set appointments. A few more would also track the number of appointments set. But even in those situations that track them both, it's not enough to effectively manage the process.

We believe that both must be tracked along with one other interim result; conversations with decision makers. Why? Because in order to help a sales professional improve at appointment-setting we need to track three metrics, not just one or two. They are:

1. The number of dials being made;

2. The number of conversations that occurred with decision makers. From the first two numbers, we can then determine the ratio between the number of dials and the number of conversations. We call it the Conversation Ratio; and

3. The number of appointments actually set with those decision makers. From this, and the number of conversations, we can determine the ratio between the number of conversations and the number of appointments set. We call this the Appointment Ratio.

Here's why we want those three metrics.

1. The number of dials being made is an indicator of effort and time management. Are they making the dials we believe they should be making or not?

2. If the Conversation Ratio is too low, there are only three reasons for it:
    a. The list they're calling off of is bad;
    b. They are not leaving voice mails and (where possible) e-mails that get returned enough; or
    c. They are struggling with gatekeepers.

3. If the Appointment Ratio is too low, there are only two reasons for that:
    a. Again the list might be bad, and the targets are not qualified; or
    b. They're not able to effectively handle the initial, "No," they'll almost invariably hear.

If our selling process truly necessitates finding new customers through telephone prospecting, accurately tracking these metrics is critical to our success. If we don't, our turnover will unnecessarily be too high (lack of early success) and our sales will be too low. Both of these negatives can be addressed if we know how to appropriately focus our effort to help our charges improve.

Lastly, the metrics must be accurate and timely. There is still only one product we're aware of that will provide that information automatically and accurately. That product is called Klpz.

COLD CALLING IS A GREAT PREDICTOR OF SALES TO COME.

So how were your sales next quarter?

The moral of this story, if you will, is that appointment making activity is a very accurate predictor of sales. If our buying cycle is ninety days as measured from an Initial Appointment, then whatever buying cycles already begun is what I will have the opportunity to close in the next ninety days.

Most managers we run into are nervously concentrating their efforts on what is going to close this month. That is obviously necessary. But to not also concentrate on the effort our sales professionals are putting into setting more buying cycles into motion this month will make us even more nervous during the month that begins two months from now.

The basic element (and therefore predictor) of an Initial Appointment is the dial. We all should be able to tell how many of those are required to generate the necessary number of Initial Appointments we need each month. We all should also be able to accurately determine how many of these precious dials are being made each day. Can you?

HOW MUCH TIME DOES IT TAKE TO SET OUR REQUIRED INITIAL APPOINTMENTS?

Why is it important to have a pretty good idea of how much time this step in the selling process should take, and how can we determine that number?

Knowing how many dials are required to hit our goals is critical. But most of us manage our day by the clock. So, how much time will it take? The answer requires us to know four metrics. If you don't know them, don't feel bad. Most people don't. Estimate them for this exercise and then start tracking your results.

1. How many Initial Appointments do we need to set?

2. The second metric is the Appointment Ratio: the number of Initial Appointments we set in relation to the number of conversations we have.

a. How *cold* are these names we're calling? (The colder and poorer the list, the more time it will take just to scrub the list for accuracy the first time through, thus requiring more attempts as our Appointment Ratio will most likely be lower.)

3. The third metric is the Conversation Ratio: the number of conversations we create in relation to the number of dials we make.

4. The fourth metric is speed: how fast can we move from dialing the first digit of phone number for target A to the dialing of the first digit of the phone number for target B. Remember, for target A, we believe we should leave a voice mail, send an e-mail if we have an address, record the results of the call, record any comments from conversations, select the date for the next call, put it away, select target B, review the history, determine where we are in our Best Practice with this particular target, and what to do on this attempt. Then, dial their number.

Our benchmarks show that on average, it takes anywhere from 2.5 minutes per dial to five or six minutes depending on our automation (or lack thereof). So let's say we need 96 Initial Appointments this year, and we have an Appointment Ratio of 25 percent and a Conversation Ratio of 8 percent. Even at five minutes per dial, I will need 109 minutes, or almost two hours per day, which is a lot for an outside sales professional. Using Klpz, that number is reduced to 55 minutes, which is much more palatable.

Most of our clients didn't realize that using spreadsheets, Outlook or CRM software to manage calling campaigns could be that expensive in terms of time. As a matter of fact, most that had invested in a CRM product thought it also aided in the prospecting process (and it does, sort of, just very inefficiently). And if we're making $100,000 per year (at about $50 per hour), that one hour saved per day is worth over $12,000 per year in lost productivity. And if that time could be invested in front of customers, the value can become substantially larger.

If you'd like a calculator to help you see how these numbers work in your environment, you can find one on our website at www. caponipg.com. It's called the Sales Activity and ROI Calculator.

WHAT DO THE LAWS OF PHYSICS AND COLD CALLING HAVE IN COMMON?

Newton's *Law of Inertia* states that, "Every object in a state of uniform motion tends to remain in that state of motion unless an external force is applied to it."

"So what does that have to do with cold calling," you ask? "Everything," I answer!

The other day, one of my customers, an independent sales professional, made an admission to me. He was new to his business and had just cranked up his cold calling regimen when he went through one of our appointment-making workshops. He quit making calls while he was taking the workshop by convincing himself that he'd develop his new process, scripts and techniques before he'd start calling again.

He just told me that he had started making calls again (over two months later), which brings me to why I brought out the *Law of Inertia*. "It was just so tough to get it going again. I used every excuse in the book," he told me.

Cold calling is not the easiest task we have to do, so human nature says we'll put it off if given a choice. But have you ever noticed that once you get doing it every day, even if it is less than you need to, it is easier each day to continue to do it. It's like my exercise routine. Once I get in the habit of doing it every day, it just seems to happen (an object in motion tends to stay in motion).

I go on a business trip and miss one or two of those habitual workout sessions and it is difficult to get back in motion again. Let's not let that happen to us in our cold calling regimen. Get in the habit of making some calls every day. If we need to make twenty, *make* the time to do it. But if we don't do twenty, then make ten calls. And if we can't do ten, do five, or three, or heck, even just a couple, but keep that object in motion!

HOW TO MOTIVATE SALES TEAMS TO MAKE COLD CALLS IN A TOUGH ECONOMY (OR ANY TIME).

All indications are that even though the economy is improving, it's still a tougher time to find prospects than we've experienced recently. With more people saying, "No," to us on cold calls, how do we keep motivated to keep making those dials?

This question came up during one of our free webinars this past week (check out www.coldcalling101.com or www.caponipg.com for a list of upcoming ones). There are three answers to that question depending on whether we're interested in addressing the symptom or the cause.

Answer No. 1 –

First of all, remember, there are only three sources of Initial Appointments which start a buying cycle: marketing programs that generate leads for us, networking and referrals, and good old fashioned cold calling. If we're not receiving enough leads and/or referrals, we have no other choice than to cold call. It is cold call or lose our job. If that's where we are, and fear is *not* how we wish to motivate, then here's an approach to put the most positive (motivating) spin on the situation.

For those of us who've been selling for a while, we'll recall the old adage of every *no* gets us closer to a *yes*, right? So here's the positive way to look at that in a cold calling environment. Divide the average size of a sale by the number of dials it takes in order to gain that sale (you'll probably have to guess in the beginning at the number of dials it takes). That will give us the value of each dial we make.

For instance, if our average sized sale is $5,000 and it takes two hundred dials to get enough Initial Appointments that result in one sale, then each time we pick up the phone and dial, it is worth $25 to us. If we can make twenty dials per hour, we're *making* $500 per hour. Not bad, eh?

Keep track of the value of those dials in a *virtual* bank. We get to withdraw the balance of our account only upon making a sale, but in the meantime, we can watch the value of our virtual bank account go up with every dial.

Another approach is to make a game out of it and come up with an incentive program for the appointments (particularly if the buying cycles are long so that the final reward is way out there).

Answer No. 2

If we really want to address the root cause of the challenge, then we've got to look at what can we do to reduce the time to make those dials (efficiency) and reduce the number of dials needed (effectiveness).

Hopefully without sounding self-serving, the ColdCalling101 solution does exactly that. Benchmarks show the efficiency component to our solution provides the ability to generally make twice the dials in the same amount of time, even if we're no better at converting those conversations we do get into appointments.

The effectiveness component steps us through a process in which we track and predict the most common negative responses and questions we're hearing. We then craft answers to those negative responses and apply the techniques of *The Formula* to counter them and turn more of them into Initial Appointments. The result is a reduction in the number of dials necessary to make a sale.

Answer No. 3

Earlier, I wrote a blog about why more civilian marathoners run farther (they'll typically finish the entire 26 miles) than Navy S.E.A.L. trainees will run who are asked to run until they can no longer feel they can go on. (It's because the civilians know where the *end* is, certainly not because those S.E.A.L. trainees are in bad shape!)

Use our Sales Activity & ROI Calculator (on the www.caponipg. com web site) to determine how many dials need be made each day. That way, at least our callers will have a goal in mind each day based on some form of logic.

And remember, nothing gets us more motivated than getting some appointments, but the toughest dial of the day is always the first.

FIVE TIPS TO HELP MAKE THAT FIRST COLD CALL OF THE DAY.

Sometimes it's hard to get started on a call block. Here are five tips.

Many times we hear the old mantra that, "Once I get started making my daily appointment-making calls, I'm okay. It's getting started that is the challenge. I'll do anything to keep from picking up that phone for the first call."

Here are five tips to help us get into the proper frame of mind to start a Call Block.

1. Read a few of customer testimonials to remind ourselves of the value we've brought to them and how pleased they are with what we deliver. Some of them are truly written from the heart, so they very motivational. I even used to have a customer I would call when I worked for HP selling computers. When I would have to make cold calls, I'd call Howard to help me get going. He loved our products and loved to talk about the new things he'd be using them for. It never failed to get me fired up.

2. Develop a calling buddy that will take a call when it's time to start a Call Block. The call can just be one of encouragement or can be a quick role-play to practice the most commonly heard negative responses.

3. Do it first and get it out of the way. This approach has another benefit—when we set appointments during our Call Block, it tends to add energy to our day.

4. Rewards--sometimes even the best of us need to be bribed. Rewarding ourselves after completing a task that we don't want to do can be effective.

5. Figure out how much each dial is worth by measuring the number of dials it takes to generate an appointment and then a sale. Each one of those dials therefore, has a value no matter whether they end in an appointment, a voice mail, or a no.

WHY IS IT IMPORTANT TO TAKE THE LONG TERM VIEW OF BUILDING TERRITORIES OVER TIME?

Here's a great way to make our job as a sales manager a little easier next year.

Sales professionals seldom take the long term view of their jobs, and hence the concept of building their territories over time is foreign to them. As sales managers, we also tend to focus on this month, this quarter, and certainly this year. It's how compensation plans are built. Companies also tend to change compensation plans and territories at the end of the year and sales professionals change companies, so it's no wonder that no one pays attention to multi-year planning and value of warming up territories over time.

I believe that it is our job as senior management to build the culture of processes and compensation plans that support the long term growth of the company. What do I mean by that? Look at your compensation plans. Do they encourage making the territory a bit warmer in the future? Even if the compensation plan doesn't explicitly encourage this approach, build appointment-setting Best Practices that support warming up targets over time.

We should leave or send consistent voice mails and e-mails that build and tell the story we want the target to understand about how our offerings have successfully been used by others. Build into those e-mails the ability for the target to request written information instead of just saying no to an appointment at the moment. Make sure to follow-up on a consistent basis by investing in technology that supports those efforts easily. Don't waste the effort being put in pursuing a particular target, even if the sales professional changes.

Why do that? Simple: next year our goal will be higher won't it? Taking the same approach year after year will finally become an overwhelming task. Trust me; we see it happen all the time. Sooner or later we pay the piper.

IS YOUR TERRITORY MORE DEFINED AND REFINED TODAY THAN IT WAS A YEAR AGO?

More on making our job as a sales manager easier in the future.

Many of us are so focused on hitting our sales target today that we forget that we're in this (or should be) for the long haul. Each year those sales targets increase, but God has not, and does not seem inclined to provide additional hours to accomplish those bigger targets. So what are we doing this year to make our task easier next year, and the year after?

When we take a look at our territory at the beginning of each year, whether it is a list of specific targeted accounts, a geographic territory or just a few major accounts, we should ask ourselves two questions about the territory itself:

1. Is my territory more refined, or warmer, than it was a year ago?

2. What can I do this year to make sure that the answer to question number one a year from now is yes?

So what do I mean by refined? If I have a brand new list of one thousand names, we know that some of these names cannot, or will not, buy from us. Our job is to not only to make sales this year, but also to continually refine that list of one thousand names, culling out the chaff and retaining the wheat for future attempts.

Many sales professionals I train work through lists of names provided them, sell to those where the timing was right, and just throw the rest of the list away and ask for more.

In past blogs, I've talked about the concept of very few of our targets being *in the market* for what we're selling when we call on them. Since we've just invested time with them on an appointment-making call only to determine they're not *in the market* right now, why not take just a few more seconds to ask an additional question or two to determine whether this is a permanent condition or just temporary?

If we do, and then ask the appropriate targets if it would be okay to call back in the future to determine if anything has changed, we're beginning to build a list of targets that have at least passed the first level of qualification. Our appointment-making task will therefore take less time next year.

BUILDING THE VALUE OF A TERRITORY OVER TIME.

More on making our job as a sales manager easier in the future.

In the past, we've talked about the value of providing a good list to our callers who must cold call. Today, we want to talk about the value of building that list over time through a well thought out Best Practice for prospecting.

If our sales team uses spreadsheets, manila folders or Big Chief yellow pads, turnover can really kill us. Those *systems* have a way of getting lost in the transition between sales professionals, even when the first person is promoted, as territory and account turnover processes generally leave a lot to be desired. Even CRMs don't work very well as they were not designed for the process that precedes the target becoming a pipeline prospect. Because of that, our sales professionals do not always enter their activity into them.

The result is the names that should be cast off are called again, and the ones that agreed to take a call again in the future can be lost, or, at best, no mention of the agreement to take a subsequent call is made. This misses the opportunity to build a Dialogue Bond[8].

During our Best Practice development process, we help sales teams design a systematic approach to calling targets on a regular basis so that over time, even if an appointment is not successfully set, the names in the territory become *warmer* for subsequent calls. And who's to say that the person who said no three months ago, but agreed to take a call again in the future, is any less qualified than a new name on a list?

Far too many sales professionals hear, "No, not now," and translate it into, "No, never," and want another name to replace the one that said no. We believe that if we ask for permission to call back again in the future to determine if things have changed, the conversations become more open and friendly over time, thus providing the platform for a substantive conversation after that Dialogue Bond is formed.

In order to make a Best Practice like that work, however, we've got to have a tool that will support it. I recommend a tool designed specifically for appointment-setting called, Klpz. You can read more about it at www.contactscience.com.

HOW CAN WE CLONE OUR BEST CUSTOMERS TO PROSPECT MORE EFFICIENTLY?

Cold calling is even tougher when we're calling someone who is not a fit. So how can we call only on companies that look like those great fits we've already sold to?

I've said it before, but let me say it again. The better our list is, the more often we'll get through to the right person and the more often we'll be able to convince that target that we've been able to help others like him or her solve like challenges.

In our ColdCalling101 Prospectors Academies, we invest time determining the top challenges our participants solve for their customers. We also get them to list the top benefits their customers tell them they derive from investing in their solution. To accomplish that, we suggest they start with their best customers in mind.

When trying to build a territory list to call from, we suggest exactly the same thing. How do we describe what our best customers look like and then go find others that look the same? Well, here are three resources we've come across that provide tools for you to enter those best customers and then *clone* them. In other words, find other companies that look just like them. They are:

- Manta.com
- InfoUSA
- Bizjournals.com (only works where the Business Journals publish)

HOW TO LEVERAGE THE CONCEPT OF DIALOGUE BONDS.

Leveraging the concept of Dialogue Bonds will both increase our dials to conversation and conversations to appointment ratios.

I talk to groups all the time about refining and warming their territories. It is done simply by asking those that tell us that are not *in the market* when we first call if we can call back again in the future to see if anything has changed. In this blog, we'll explore in a little bit more depth how that works to our advantage.

Rest assured that when we first call someone their initial reaction is guarded at best. We are a stranger, we are interrupting them, and we're trying to sell them something they don't think they need at the moment. However, an interesting thing happens over time if we ask for permission to call back and then do so.

If we call this person again as promised, we will begin to develop what a friend of mine, Bill Wallace, calls the Dialogue Bond. It may not be on the second call, and maybe not even on the third, but sooner or later, they'll remember us and the tone in their voice will be much more warm and welcoming. That will provide us the opportunity to get into a conversation where we can share how we've helped others in their position. And more importantly, they'll listen because they *know* us.

The moral of the story? Prospecting and cold calling has a cumulative effect. Ask for permission to call back and then do it. Most also find that our cold calls are actually more enjoyable as well.

AN EXAMPLE OF THE CUMULATIVE EFFECT OF PROSPECTING.

Be in it for the long run. Have a well defined Cycle for calling and stick with it because appointment-making has a cumulative effect over time.

When I do not get an appointment (and unless I believe the target will never become a prospect), I always ask if it's okay if I call back again in six months to see if anything has changed. I have never had a single person say no to that.

This past week, I called a sales manager that I have been calling for four years, every six months (my Klpz appointment-setting tool shows thirty-two steps during that time). As a matter of fact, when I introduced myself on this last call, you would have thought I was talking to an old friend. That's an example of what I call the Dialogue Bond I've discussed in previous blogs (also defined in the Glossary). We had a, "How you doing?" or, "How you doin?" (for my New Jersey friends) type conversation just like friends would prior to *him starting the business portion of the call with*, "I'm glad you called. Things have changed and I need you."

I also interject some of these follow-up calls into my regular cold calling call blocks and it certainly doesn't hurt the confidence level to listen to a voice that is open to the conversation.

ANOTHER THOUGHT ON THE CUMULATIVE EFFECT OF PROSPECTING.

They say that numbers can be made to support just about any position. "Figures don't lie, but liars figure."But here's a set of numbers we should pay attention to. They are statistics about how often we sales professionals follow up.

In earlier blogs, I have provided examples of the cumulative value of prospecting and how a Dialogue Bond develops over time with a target that has yet to grant us an appointment. It's a simple case of three things; being persistent about following up, applying the appropriate *Art* professionally on each call which allows us to qualify a little more on each of those calls, and having an enabling technology that allows us to do so efficiently. (Don't let those follow-up calls fall through the cracks--they're more valuable than we think.) Here's some sales *statistics* to back that up:

- 48 percent of sales people never follow-up with a prospect
- 25 percent of sales people make a second contact and stop
- 12 percent of sales people only make three contacts and stop
- Only 10 percent of sales people make more than three attempts

And

- 2 percent of sales are made on the first contact
- 3 percent of sales are made on the second contact
- 5 percent of sales are made on the third contact

- 10 percent of sales are made on the fourth contact
- 80 percent of sales are made on the fifth to twelfth contact

What makes us think that a first call to someone else will be more effective than a subsequent call to someone we've tried before when the statistics actually bear out the opposite? We must have a plan (we call them Ideal Pursuit Plans or Cycles). How many times will we attempt to reach someone, how often will we make those attempts and then what kind of time period will we allow to elapse before putting them through another Cycle. The activity itself (the planning, the calling, the recording, reporting, etc.) can be time consuming and fraught with opportunities for us to lose track of our progress.

ANOTHER REASON WHY INVESTING TIME AND EFFORT INTO THE CREATION OF OUR COLD CALLING LISTS IS SO IMPORTANT.

When we deliver our Prospector's Academies, sales management is responsible to provide each sales professional in the program with a list of targets to call. In too many cases, this is an afterthought and done at the last minute.

In a recent program, one team threw 80 percent of the names they processed off the list after their first call of the Cycle. In addition to the normal out of business and bad numbers, these companies were too small, too big, didn't use what they sold, etc. That is very frustrating for the sales professional and expensive for sales management.

Part of the Coldcalling101 solution is a tool called Klpz (www.contactscience.com). Klpz provides calling metrics; one of them being the number and percentage of removals. Since the sales professional will also supply a short description of why the target being removed, it provides invaluable information regarding the quality of lists.

When a sales professional makes the required number of dials yet doesn't get the appointments you expected, can you tell why?

Our customers can and there are a number of variables—including the quality of the list.

Very few of us have more money and time than we know what to do with, so we recommend that you invest time studying your best current customer profile and then looking for lists that mirror those. We also suggest that you measure the effectiveness of your calling programs so that you can improve them.

FOUR QUESTIONS TO ASK OURSELVES TO DETERMINE WHETHER TO APPLY SALES 2.0 TECHNIQUES TO THE APPOINTMENT-SETTING PROCESS.

The Sales 2.0 Methodology is another one of those approaches that is supposed to eliminate the need for cold calling. But as with just about everything in life, there are caveats.

I just read a very good e-book by Nigel Edelshain, originator of Sales 2.0 Methodology. In it he talks about all of the excellent tools or processes that are now available to us to research our targets, or use them to get an introduction to the person we wish to speak with. Examples are Linkedin, triggers of events, Jigsaw, and ZoomInfo.

All are good ideas, but here's the operative question we must ask ourselves prior to engaging the Sales 2.0 approach. Is it worth it to do all of this work prior to picking up the phone and asking for an appointment?

Shame on us if we set an Initial Appointment with someone, yet do not research them prior to *attending* the meeting with them. Don't get me wrong, I am a big proponent of the Sales 2.0 process prior to trying to set the appointment with the appropriate target. But it is not applicable in every selling environment. To spend an hour, or even thirty minutes, researching every target in our territory when our average sized sale is small and we're selling commodities can be counter-productive. If our territory is very large, and our typical target is pretty homogenous, it can also be a waste of time.

So here are four questions we should ask ourselves before deciding to do a lot of research prior to attempting to set an appointment.

1. What is my average size sale or what is the lifetime value of this potential customer?
2. What do I sell (how complex a sale is it)?
3. How big is my universe of targets?
4. What level of management am I calling into?

If our average sale is small, if our solution is a simple commodity and/ or our solution is sold into a *horizontal* market, we may eat up most of our profit in a lot of up front investigative time. To make my point, let me use an example at the other end of the spectrum. Let's say our average size sale is more than $50,000 and we only have one hundred possible targets in our territory. In that instance, we can't afford to *not be* prepared when we speak with our target executive on the phone. We're therefore going to be doing all of the networking, research, social media, etc. to make sure we don't blow it when we actually try to get the person on the phone to set the appointment.

In those *not-worth it* situations, we prefer to invest our time just *once* in building a solid approach script, voice mails and e-mails that tell the story of how we helped someone else like them, and then work on how we handle the inevitable *no* we still get when asking for the appointment the first time.

At the end of the day, when we place that call, we're still trying to set an appointment with someone we don't know, or have just barely met. And just because we did a lot of research and even got a strong referral, our experience still dictates that we're still going to hear exactly the same types of *no*. They'll just be nicer about it. We've still got to have the skills to counter that *no*.

Those topics are covered in depth in Volume I: Effectiveness, the Art of Appointment Making.

TO CANVAS OR NOT, IS THE QUESTION MY DEAR WATSON. TEN QUESTIONS TO ASK OURSELVES TO DETERMINE THE ANSWER.

When does it make sense to hop in the car and burn some shoe leather versus using the phone to prospect?

The price of gas has come down off its highs of 2008, but the cost of an hour of our time has not.

Should we canvas for Initial Appointments or use the phone? In pure cold calling environments, it's a question that gets asked a lot. So what's the answer? We believe that it depends on how we answer the following questions:

1. How experienced are our sales professionals and how comfortable are they at picking up the phone and calling for an appointment? The less comfortable, the more canvassing makes sense as many inexperienced sales professionals seem to find it easier to pick up the phone and make a subsequent call into a company they've physically visited.

2. How many new names do we need to add to our target list each month? If it is a lot, attaining lists makes more sense as canvassing takes a lot of time.

3. Are we prospecting into a zip code or something larger? If we've got a multi-state territory, canvassing is problematic.

4. Do we practice vertical prospecting, or are we geographic in focus? Canvassing makes more sense in a horizontal selling environment where we can march down the block and find targets.

5. How much are we out on the street anyway? If we are out and about every day, or at least three days a week, then

building in some time to canvas can also makes sense. (Also see number 8.)

6. How much would the receptionist, or the person we'd contact face-to-face, know about what we need to uncover about a target? The more common that information within the organization (or at least with the person we'd mostly encounter), the more canvassing makes sense.

7. Security challenges. In New York City for instance, canvassing can't work as security precludes us from getting into many buildings without an invitation.

8. What is the average size of our sale? There is a correlation between the cost of making a sale and the value of the sale. Canvassing is more expensive when one takes into account the cost of driving around and the cost of our time. Related to the average size of our sale is the concept of recurring orders. If our sale is small but will result in reorders over time, canvassing can make sense even when the revenue gained from one sale is small. Also, as mentioned in point number 5, if we are out on the street anyway, and need to stop by existing customers to cross sell and up-sell, it can make sense.

9. What is the level of person we're trying to reach? This is related to the average size of our sale. The bigger the ticket, the higher the level of person we need to see. The higher the level of the person we wish to see, particularly in larger organizations, the less likely they are to grant us an appointment when canvassing. They are also easier to identify when purchasing a list.

10. What is the size of the organization we're calling on? If we're calling on retail or small businesses where everyone is at one location, canvassing can make sense. If we're calling on large businesses with multiple locations,

finding the person we need to meet with may be a waste of time.

WHY WON'T JOHNNY USE OUR CRM (CUSTOMER RELATIONSHIP MANAGEMENT SOFTWARE) TO TELEPHONE PROSPECT?

Companies spend untold amounts of money implementing CRM applications. There are multiple reasons why CRM does not help in the process of setting Initial Appointments with new business targets.

The simple answer to our question is that CRMs were not built to automate the business process of telephone prospecting. They were built to handle customer relationships and pipeline management. They are very good at that, and for those of us who have any kind of installed base, necessary.

The better question to ask is why we continue to use them to set appointments. The answer to that question is a combination of:

- We view CRM as the Swiss Army knife of sales tools;
- The CRM is already in place;
- We were told it handled that when we bought it (and it does, but so poorly that many sales professionals just don't use it for that purpose—or worse, don't prospect enough because it is so cumbersome and, hence, painful);
- The lack of use of the CRM for prospecting is lumped in with the lack of CRM use in general; and, lastly
- And this is the biggest reason—we don't really grasp that prospecting is a process; therefore we don't appreciate the real role of automation in its success.

This is a big topic for us, so we've continued to study it for years. We believe that we've correctly defined telephone prospecting as a business process. This process requires us to assemble the correct combination of Art, Best Practice and Science to be successful. That's right, without getting all three business process components correct, we fail.

The purpose of the Science component is to provide efficiency. Specifically, it allows sales professionals to quickly, easily, and accurately navigate their Best Practices while in the simultaneous pursuit of potentially hundreds of targets. It must also automatically report on that prospecting activity.

CRMs are not only inefficient in this role; they are proven during benchmarks to be counter-productive. For instance, it takes at least twice as long and takes 85 percent more effort (see table below) to follow the typical Best Practice for telephone prospecting in a CRM than it does in Klpz.

This table represents the results we've gotten from a number of benchmarks we've performed with customers who have optimized their CRM for prospecting.

Application	Clicks	Screens	Time
Klpz	42	11	18 minutes
Salesforce	260	126	48 minutes
Goldmine	301	151	50 minutes
ACT!	312	150	53 minutes

Regardless of what we think about the added mouse clicks, key board entries and thought that must go into the process, the important column to pay attention to is the far right. Sales is a results oriented endeavor. I've mentioned it in many other blogs—we have only so many hours in each day. To be successful in sales, we must not only be effective, but we must also be efficient.

It is a very painless (and free) process to benchmark a CRM. If you're interested, send an e-mail to Bob Howard at Contact Science. He can be reached at bhoward@klpz.com.

ABOUT THE AUTHOR

Mr. Caponi is the president and founder of Caponi Performance Group, Inc., a sales consulting and training company located in the Dallas, Texas, area.

His company focuses on assisting its clients increase top-line revenue by assisting its sales teams to get in front of more targets in less time. That is accomplished through its brand, ColdCalling101™, which combines the company's own skills methodology or *Art*, called *The Appointment Making Formula™*, along with Klpz, a web-based specialized prospecting application, known as the *Science*, from Contact Science, LLC.

Mr. Caponi brings over twenty-five years of broad management, sales, and sales management experience to his business. His general management experience includes responsibility for a regional property management firm and worldwide P&L responsibility as a general manager for a division of a software company. On the sales side, in addition to a successful career as a salesperson, he has run local, North American, and global sales teams.

His industry experience includes computer hardware and software, and telecommunications as well as getting his sales start selling life and health insurance. He's worked for multi-billion dollar companies such as Hewlett-Packard and Computer Associates, mid-sized companies such as MetaSolv (now Oracle) of Plano, Texas, as well as his share of start-ups.

Mr. Caponi has closed business in his career that ranged from small deals measured in the thousands of dollars to large deals valued between $30M and $50M. Mr. Caponi has had articles on sales published all across the world in addition to his hometown publications such as the *Dallas Morning News* and the *Dallas Business Journal.*

He can be reached by e-mail at bcaponi@caponipg.com or through his website at www.caponipg.com.

GLOSSARY

Having a common language is important for understanding. In sales, many of the terms that we use are interchangeable, making communication and understanding difficult at best. Have you ever been in a pipeline review session where *prospect* was used to describe someone who had just been identified as potentially a good future customer to pursue—and then, seconds later, the same term was used to describe someone who is almost closed?

Many of the companies that we have helped use different terminology to describe the same things, so here's a glossary of the terms we use in this book:

Art. We use this term to describe the set of skills used to get through to the decision-maker more often and turn more of those conversations into appointments.

Best Practice. We use this term to describe a particular component of Art and/or Science that is adopted by the organization as the de facto way of doing something. Examples of Best Practices are target acquisition approaches, territory building strategy, Cycle or target pursuit designs, the process we'll use to pursue a target over the life cycle of that target, and the messaging we'll deliver when speaking with the target or should we need to leave a message.

Buying Cycle. We use this term to describe what most call a Sales Cycle. We like our term because it is the Prospect—not us—that controls it, regardless of how we want to kid ourselves.

Call Block. We use this term to describe a block of time set aside to make appointment-setting calls.

Conditioned Knee-Jerk Responses. We use this term to describe how most people respond when they are cold called. The important thing to understand is that this is almost always a reflex action. All of us have our favorite way that we get a sales professional off the phone or away from our front door. Generally, it has nothing to do with reality. Also see negative responses.

Counters. We use this term to describe the specific process we have designed within **The Formula** to address the negative response that we generally receive when we ask for an appointment.

Customer. We use this term for consistency. Some companies use other terms such as client, guest, etc. There is no particular importance to be gleaned from our selection of this term.

Cycle. We use this term to describe the framework we define as an adopted Best Practice for the pursuit of a particular class of targets. It contains the type of attempt to contact (snail mail, e-mail, canvas, or phone call), number of attempts we will make before putting this target away again for some predetermined time, frequency of those attempts, and what that predetermined time is before we begin the Cycle again should we be unable to connect during this Cycle.

Dialogue Bond. Coined by a good friend, Bill Wallace, of Dallas, we use this term to describe the phenomena of almost friendship that occurs after talking with someone numerous times over the phone— even if the two parties have never met. This is one of the reasons why we believe that prospecting has a cumulative effect.

Ideal Pursuit Plan. See *Cycle.*

Initial Appointment. We use this term to define a first meeting with a target (not yet a Prospect) in which we (the target *and* us) will attempt to jointly determine whether they are willing and able to become a Prospect for the particular solution we wish to currently sell to them. It could actually be an existing customer for which we will attempt to up-sell or cross-sell, but more typically is someone that we've never met.

In the market. We use this term to refer to someone who realizes a need or desire to solve a challenge and are actively pursuing a resolution. It is an important concept because when we prospect, surveys show that more than 95 percent of our universe of potential targets do not think that they are in the market when we call them.

Move on Message. The last voice mail message in the Cycle of calls that informs the target this will be the last time we call for a while. It generally elicits the largest number of returned voice mails.

Negative Responses. We use this term to describe the different categories of no that we hear when our targets respond to us when we ask for an Initial Appointment. There are only four categories and they are:

- Already have what you sell
- Don't need what you sell

- Don't have time
- Send me something

(Also see Conditioned Knee-Jerk Response.)

Pattern Interruption. We use this term to describe the unorthodox order that we suggest supplying information to a gatekeeper when they take a message for us. The order we use interrupts the pattern they are used to thinking in and reduces the risk of them asking for a more detailed description of the purpose for the call.

Pipeline Phase of the Selling Process. We believe that there are two distinct components to the selling process. The Pipeline Phase begins generally at the end of the Initial Appointment when we, and the target, agree that it makes sense to enter into a buying cycle. It is at this stage the target becomes a *Prospect.*

Prospect. See Pipeline Phase of the Selling Process and Initial Appointment.

Sales professional. We use this term to describe what most call the Sales Rep or Account Exec. We believe that sales is a profession— hence our choice of the term.

Selling Ratios

   Appointment Ratio. The number of Initial Appointments divided by the number of conversations (with the person we want the appointment with) had attaining those appointments.

   Conversation Ratio. The number of conversations divided by the number of dials required to attain those conversations.

Close Ratio. The number of sales closed divided by the number of Initial Appointments. (We realize that some people calculate this by using proposals generated as the denominator, but we like this definition for a variety of reasons beyond the scope of this book.)

Target. We use this term to describe the entity and/or the person we've defined as being someone that could use and afford our solution. We do use the word Prospect, but only after we've met with them and together, we've agreed that they are willing and able to enter into a typical Buying Cycle.

OTHER RESOURCES

In the Introduction, I referenced two white papers that I have written that can also help you with this topic. In several blogs, I also mentioned a Sales Activity and ROI Calculator. For those and more on ColdCalling101™ and *The Appointment Making Formula™*, visit the following websites. Also look for a follow-up book from me in late 2011 that will be a full how-to book.

- Caponi Performance Group, Inc.—www.caponipg.com
- Contact Science, LLC—www.contactscience.com
- Blog—www.coldcalling101.com/blog
- YouTube—www.youtube.com/coldcalling101

Although I do not agree with all of the techniques and approaches in the following resources, there are some very good concepts for specific issues that we can all face, depending on our selling environment. For instance, if you're selling into large companies, take a look at *The Power to Get In*. Michael Boylan suggests calling into multiple entry points and letting each know that you're calling into the others. His theory on that is terrific. If you've got a very finite number of targets to sell to, read *Selling to Vito*. Anthony Parinello addresses upfront work before you pick up the phone.

The only three methodologies I mentioned in the Introduction that I at least somewhat agree with are *Cold Calling Techniques, Knock Your Socks Off Prospecting,* and *Red-Hot Cold Call Selling.* Again, I do not agree with all of their concepts, but overall, I think that they have some great ideas and techniques that you can benefit from.

The first resource on the following list is a pretty interesting one. It is a discussion group on LinkedIn dedicated to this topic. You can find some great questions being asked and read some really different approaches to answering those questions. You can then make up your mind as to what might work in your environment.

Here's the full list of resources on appointment-setting:

- LinkedIn Discussion Group—Best Practices for Telephone Prospecting/Cold Calling
- Stephen Schiffman—*Cold Calling Techniques (That Really Work!)*
- William "Skip" Miller and Ron Zemke—*Knock Your Socks Off Prospecting*
- Paul S. Goldner—*Red-Hot Cold Call Selling*
- Anthony Parinello—*Selling to Vito (the Very Important Top Officer)*
- Michael A. Boylan—*The Power To Get In*

The following two resources have had a great impact on our Art methodology. We provide copies of Dr. Cialdini's *Influence* CD to our Prospector's Academy students since it is one of the best overall selling pieces we've run across. It will help you in all phases of selling—not to mention all of your dealings with people. I have customers tell me all the time that they still carry Robert's CD in their car and listen to it over and over.

Neuro-Linguistic Programming is all about choosing the right words (and avoiding the wrong ones) based on studies of how the mind works. Jim Fortin's workshops are the best.

Lastly, Dorothy Leed's *The 7 Powers of Questions* is not a sales book, but it is the best book on questions I've come across. Her concepts apply to all areas of our lives: selling, family, work, everything. Great book.

The particulars on those resources:

- Dr. Robert Cialdini—Studies of why people have the tendency to comply with the requests of others, www.influenceatwork.com
- Jim Fortin, Neuro-Linguistic Programming research and concepts, www.mindauthority.com
- Dorothy Leeds, *The 7 Powers of Questions*

ENDNOTES

1. (This is the script for a cartoon I saw years ago. My apologies to the author for not properly crediting him/her, but I couldn't find his or her name.)

2. The tool we use is called Klpz, from Contact Science, LLC, located in Memphis, TN

3. See Top Ten Biggest Mistakes Cold Callers Make on the phone – No. 1

4. See Top Ten Biggest Mistakes Cold Callers Make on the phone – No. 1

5. See www.caponipg.com to download a free one.

6. See glossary for definition.

7. See www.caponipg.com to download a free one.

8. See Glossary for definition.